W9-CRV-931

CONVERSATIONS WITH TOMORROW

ACHIEVING ENVIRONMENTAL BALANCE

The Fairns

CONVERSATIONS WITH TOMORROW
ACHIEVING ENVIRONMENTAL BALANCE
by The Fairns
speaking through Jasmine Contor

Published by: **CDC Publishing**
216 Redwood Avenue
Willits, California 95490

All rights reserved. No part of this book may be reproduced or transmitted in any form or means without written permission from one of the authors, except for brief quotations that are part of a review.

Copyright (c) 1993 by Jasmine Contor
First printing second edition 1993
Printed in the United States of America
Cover design by Dan Dawson
Cover Graphics by Tom Jarvis
Fairns channeled by Jasmine Contor
Primary questioners Jim and Kitsy Dunham
Edited by Lu Ransom and Jasmine Contor
Initiated by Fred Steele and Jim Dunham

Publication Data
Conversations with Tomorrow - Acheiving Environmental Balance
by The Fairns
New age / Environment
ISBN 0-9632967-0-1: $14.95 Softcover

CONVERSATIONS WITH TOMORROW
ACHIEVING ENVIRONMENTAL BALANCE

TABLE OF CONTENTS

ACKNOWLEDGEMENTS

This book is the result of the support given by the many people who have spoken with The Fairns over the years. I would especially like to thank Lu Ransom, Jim and Kitsy Dunham, Fred and Sandy Steele, Lauren and Larry Rocha, Linda and Perry Desiante, John Caire III and Dan Dawson.

Jasmine Contor

In accordance with Beneficial Wholism Assessment, this book is printed on one hundred percent recycled paper.

My first experience with channeling was a group session with Jasmine and The Fairns. At the time I was skeptical. Having a scientific background and an interest in physics, I decided to ask about Field Theory. It was quite a surprise that The Fairns[1] were able to address the subject in even a general way. I attended several more sessions that year. The people talked about everything from past lives to what was wrong with their horses. By being in those sessions, I picked up a feeling for the Fairns abilities, knowledge, and their tremendous respect for the individual. It became apparent that they were an incredible source of information. At that time I did not know the extent of The Fairns abilities and limitations that are covered in the second chapter of this the book. Subsequently, I discovered some interesting facts. One factor which affects the type of information is the perspective of the Entity sending the information. For example, Entities which have recently evolved out of the Physical experience will have a different perspective than a large group Entity which is far along the evolutionary path and able to impact causality directly. To my knowledge, The Fairns are one of the more evolutionarily advanced group Entities being channeled. While this is exceptional with regards to perspective and information access, there are obstacles to overcome in the process. We have problems making decisions based on our own memory and "here and now" facts. Imagine the problems facing an Entity which stretches out not only in space but also in time. Imagine observing all "Nows" simultaneously or communicating from that perspective to a single moving moment in time. Being farther along the evolutionary path means bridging a greater gap to communicate to the Physical world. It also means carrying a greater weight of responsibility. All of this makes Jasmine a very special person; a person who can maintain the required blank state and bridge the gap which connects to The Fairns.

Many people realize that our planet is in trouble and want to help with the healing. We decided it would be productive to put The Fairns' perspective to good use by discussing the environment and publishing the observations. We wanted "nuts and bolts" answers; information about what is going on and how to heal the planet's wounds. The information, of course, has to be put into context. We were quite

---

[1]Fairns - A composite entity that speaks through Jasmine Contor.

surprised at how complex and yet specific the context turned out to be.

If even a small number of people absorb the information we have gathered and act on it, they will make a large contribution. This type of information brings a dawn of new physics, and as so will encounter the inertia of existing doctrine. That is just human nature. Eventually, as in the past, the experiments and experience will filter the wheat from the chaff.

There are several very controversial pieces of information in this book that the reader can assess over the next few decades. One is that the whales, especially the larger species, are much more advanced spiritually than humans. Their "intelligence" and ensoulment will become increasingly apparent. There are also impending discoveries of materials such as plastic-steel and plastic-ceramics combinations. Of course there is no amount of evidence that will satisfy or prove everything to everyone. Much of the material in this book is unprovable. Each individual can decide on the basis of his/her feelings whether it seems correct.

The other aspect of this material that was not anticipated at the onset is the potential for individuals to rediscover, by themselves, the many seemingly lost abilities of Mind Mechanics. When one experiences the recovery of such abilities then the knowing becomes direct. The reality of such abilities is no longer a hypothetical potential to be accepted on faith, but a direct experience. There are many people who can apply the hints in this material to their own development and to the enlivening of our Mother Planet. As this book and others like it grow in impact, there will be many people spending a large amount of energy trying to prove that reality is not what it really is. It is important not to waste a great deal of energy arguing over different points of view. Instead, concentrate on understanding and putting the information into action. The results will be apparent for all to observe. **Conversations with Tomorrow** allows you to act in fore-sight with the advantage of hind-sight.

Jim Dunham

Glossary of Unconventional Terms

Tao (Dow) - Whole of the Whole, All That Is, Supreme Being.

Shis - she/he, his/hers. The Fairns do not make gender distiction.

Enedswr (en-ed-ez-ware) - human being, or any species which is conscious of self; any species with a soul.

House - body.

House-self - animal body instincts.

Soul-in-house - soul and body combined.

Soul pattern - soul; that part of a being which is eternal.

Hive - animal; also any animal species which has a group soul.

Play - life outline; life design, or potential design.

Maya - illusion; social accultruation and/or endoctrination; handed down belief systems.

Stretchy/Stretching - difficult; taxing; challenging.

INTRODUCTION

Conversations with Tomorrow is a series of discussions with The Fairns, a group Mental Plane Entity. In 1983 the first collection of Fairns material was made available to the public in the form of the Tao Song newsletters. At The Fairns suggestion this material has been incorporated into Conversations with Tomorrow to give the reader a better understanding of the "Greater Reality." It provides a foundation for the main thrust of the book, which centers on the environment. The information in the Tao Song newsletters explains our responsibility for the environmental situation by outlining a definitive explanation of the inner workings of the Universe.

The Fairns are very knowledgeable and have the ability to deal in specifics. However, a complete detailing of the environmental situation is well beyond the focus of any individual book, including this one. The larger contents of this book are selected topics on environmental problems and an overview. The focus is on what is not known and how to improve the situation. This book is a valuable asset for the action oriented person committed to healing the Planet. The first words received from The Fairns were:

"Tao Song."

JASMINE

The Fairns are channeled through Jasmine Contor, whom they affectionately call, "This One." Asked why they chose Jasmine as their channel, they relayed that she made a pre-life choice to do so and, in her physical Now, maintains the clarity needed for their transmissions. "We usurped her," they concluded.

Raised by parents who were teachers with a passion for the arts, Jasmine studied music and dance. She became a professional violinist and an accomplished dancer. In 1979, she turned to sculpture as an outlet for her talents and was able to support herself by selling her unique, detailed porcelain creations.

She was five when she first saw her "Rainbow People," who she now knows were Non-physical Plane Beings.

"It was summertime. I was sitting in my Sunday School class gazing through the open classroom door. Suddenly, I saw little beings on the grass beckoning me to come play. Oblivious to my startled teacher and surprised classmates, I ran out to join the "Rainbow People" in the churchyard.

"They made no sound, but I 'heard' them perfectly when they told me, 'Reach up and grab the sunshine. Roll it in a ball and play with us.' It was easy as making a snowball and soon we were throwing balls of sunshine at each other. They hit me more often than I hit them, but when one of my sunshine balls found its target, the ball burst into shards of color and notes of beautiful music. We splashed the sunshine . . . it's impossible to describe."

During the following year, at least once-a-week, when she was playing in the yard, three Rainbow People appeared and joined her in a game of sunshine ball. Many years passed before she learned these beings were teachers, assigned to tune her energy and vibrations to the Rate (speed, vibration, or intensity) and Function of the Fairns.

After the Rainbow People left, Jasmine began hearing voices in her head. In grammar school, those voices confused her when she was learning 1+1=2, 2+2=4, 4+4=8, etc.. Laughing hysterically, they said, "How silly! 1+1=3, 2+2=5, 4+4=9," finally convincing her that what her teacher called even numbers were really odd, and odd numbers were even (the progression is consistent with adding one to every sum). Because she believed what her voices said, she has always had difficulty with conventional arithmetic.

When Jasmine was in her twenties, her mother, Lu, an avid reader of psychology and philosophy, delved into metaphysics. She shared her interest with her sister, June. Soon, both were reading and exchanging metaphysical books. During the summer of 1979, while Lu was visiting her, June went into a bookstore in search of something "light" to read. As she wandered along the shelves, a book literally fell into her hands. Startled, she skimmed the "blurb" on the cover. When she discovered its contents dealt with channeling through a Ouija board, she bought it. They were intrigued by the author's revelations about contacting metaphysical beings through a Ouija board. Lu evinced a desire for her own copy, but when June returned to the bookstore for another, she couldn't find one on the shelf. When she asked the manager for another copy, he told her he had never stocked the book, and had never heard of it.

Flabbergasted, June reported her experience to Lu. After much conjecture, the two decided someone or something might be trying to contact them. Feeling stupid and foolish they got a Ouija board. The moment their fingers touched it, messages came. The communicants identified themselves as a group of Entities referred to as The Fairns. One message predominated: "Get Jasmine. We can speak through her."

When Lu returned to California, she took the Ouija board with her. After much cajoling, Jasmine agreed to participate in the "game." In moments, The Fairns were answering questions as fast as Lu could record them. Though they kept assuring Jasmine the Ouija board was an unnecessary crutch, that they needed only her voice, she remained skeptical. For almost a year, she refused to channel without the board.

Finally, The Fairns assuaged her concern of influencing their messages by acquiescing to her demand that she be in full trance and remember nothing of what they said. They suggested she get a clear leaded crystal pyramid to help her move into trance, telling her a leaded crystal was necessary because the Rate of their vibrations through her body would shatter a natural crystal.

"The moment I look in that crystal, I'm gone. It never ceases to amaze me. Within five to ten seconds, I am somewhere else. Listeners tell me The Fairns start speaking in a scratchy voice that sounds like four of five people speaking at the same time with "froggy" throats."

"It's difficult to describe where I go. When I look into the crystal, a light goes on inside and I move toward it. I sense The Fairns coming. I get a vague impression, more of a feeling, of a combination of colors, motion, and sound. Colors like fireworks, sound like music, and whirling motion."

"I wait in a lighted room, consciously unaware of where I am, without physical sensations, but not asleep. Like being in suspended animation. On hold."

"When they finish speaking through me, the light goes out in the "waiting" room and comes on in my physical body. I come toward that light, and they pass on their way out. I get a general impression, a sense, of what they feel, whether they're pleased or excited, but I know if I tune in consciously and observe how they look as we pass, I would be unable to tolerate the intensity of their energy. I would burn up. So I catch a quick glimpse, like a flash in reflective glass. Most of the time, I feel very warm when I come back, though the degree of warmth varies. Sometimes, I feel rejuvenated and full of energy. Other times, I feel incredibly depleted. I think it depends on the person The Fairns have been talking to and the subject matter discussed. Following trance state, I need time to clear and to "ground" after I return to the Physical Plane."

"My understanding of this process is that I have the ability to be a "telephone" for Non-physical Plane Entities, and The Fairns selected me as their "private" line."

"People ask me The Fairns purpose for their inter-plane communications. I believe they communicate with those here to reassure us that we are not alone, that we do not live out short physical lives and die, that there are many levels of Being."

"They claim they are not allowed to say anything to influence the "seeker's" decisions. They tell me, "Guidance does not interfere with an individual's free will to make shis own decisions. We suggest. We do not command." But they will not suggest the winning lottery number or the specific outcomes of possible choices."

"Being a "private line" for The Fairns is an extra-ordinary gift. Though it is sometimes disturbing and uncomfortable, it is also my purpose and my joy. I continue to be surprised and amazed when people tell me what The Fairns say, but I am grateful they can speak through me. I feel blessed."

The Fairns speak through Jasmine to give us Power and Positive Energy and to remind us that the first Law of The Tao is: **All is One.** During the last thirteen years, through Jasmine, they have brought comfort, understanding and purpose to the lives of hundreds of people. They have united us in Positive Action for our Planet, and empowered us to relieve our anxiety and fear with Positive Action. Through on-going conversations with The Fairns, we expand our understanding that we are all an essential part of the "Whole of the Whole," the "All Loving Force".

Tao Song.

WHO ARE YOU, FAIRNS?

Before we get into the specifics of the environment, we want to provide a basis for the information. We need to establish that your perspective is consistent with the type of information given. To this end, it is important to define the extent of your abilities and limitations. Could you describe your self to the readers? Who you are?

Sometimes this can be more confusing than enlightening. However, we will do the best we can with words.

We are a composite group of what, in your terms, you call people or individuals.

We must digress briefly to put this in context. Each person has an individual Soul Pattern. These individual Patterns reincarnate in the Physical Plane until their learning is completed. Once individual Patterns complete Physical Plane function, they gradually unite to become a larger whole.

Now, our form or Rate[2] of Being we define as a Larger Entity. Entities who function at this Rate are comprised of from one thousand to fifteen hundred individual Soul Patterns which are finished reincarnating in Physical Plane form. Our composite being includes two of these Larger Entities. We work together and confer together. There is a dominate vocal aspect and that is what you are hearing through Jasmine. One Entity of our composite is functioning at one Rate. The second is functioning at a slightly different Rate.

If you wish to explain this in terms that are more familiar, you could say we exist on the "Mental" plane. This does not mean "mental" in your terms of definition. It is just a name. Mental Plane is the sixth Plane. Subsequent there is the seventh Plane and then The Tao, the Entirety. One Entity of which we are comprised functions at the second level Mental Plane. The other functions at seventh level Mental Plane. The Entity of second level of the Mental Plane is E'sef (pronounce E' as in Ever) and the seventh level is E'fairn. The original name is E'sef E'fairn which we have shortened to Fairns which is much easier to say.

---

[2]Rate - an undefined term, the best feeling inference is vibration or speed.

This may seem extraneous in terms of description. However, we function with the cumulative knowledge of nearly three thousand individual Soul Patterns. We have the combined experience of their lifetimes and have access to their learning. Our job, you might say, is to assist those workers and Searchers who realize there are other Rates of consciousness and existence besides the Physical Plane. This of course means you. People who are Searchers can feel within themselves their connection to the greater Whole, or The Tao, as we prefer to say.

In your society, the society of Western Civilization, the Judeo-Christian ethic is strong. If the word "God" is used people evoke an image of a kindly old man with a profuse white beard - a personification of their, you might say, Grandfather! We use the term Tao as this is a word which is neutral in meaning for Western culture.

We are not permitted to interfere with Physical Plane function or interrupt any individual's free choice or free will.

On what Plane do we reside, in comparison to where you are?

You are residing in the Physical Plane, which is the first Plane. Then there is the Astral Group: Lower Astral, Middle Astral, and Upper Astral which are counted as planes two, three, and four. The Causal Plane is five. Then Mental, which is the sixth Plane. This Plane has seven levels or Rates within itself. Then Buddhic Plane, then The Tao. Of course, you must remember that this explanation is stated in a linear form for your comprehension. In the Greater Reality there are no such rigid divisions.

The three Planes comprising the Astral Group are sometimes referred to as the Astral Plane, and this can be a source of confusion. The Astral Group is the main source of tangible contact with the Physical Plane. The Lower Astral is reserved for Souls who have recently passed from the Physical Plane. The Middle Astral is for counselling of and preparation by Souls between lives for their return to the Physical Plane.[3]

Why have you come to speak with us?

Your desire to know Truth allows us to teach and that is why we come to you.

You have a job, which implies duties and responsibilities. Who

---

[3]Also see Chapter Three -"The Structure of the Greater Reality".

coordinates these? Is it The Tao, The Entirety?

We consult and coordinate directly with three Buddhic Entities. Buddhic Entities function at the seventh Plane Rate or speed. One of the three is a Taoic Will Translator. So, though that may be opening more incomprehensible questions, with reservation we would say, yes, we can receive direct Taoic intents. We wish to make one thing quite clear. Though we can receive communications and information, this does not necessarily mean that we can comprehend The Tao in its totality. Only the Whole of the Whole itself can completely comprehend the totality of itself. So, from your perspective it is a one way communication system. The Taoic Will is sent; we receive.

So you can request information from the source, like we can request information from you.

Yes, that is correct. Or we can hear and receive but not necessarily comprehend the totality of The Taoic Mind.

Who are the other two Buddhic Plane Entities and would you describe their function?

It is as difficult to describe the beings of the Buddhic Plane and the extent of their function as it is for us to describe or comprehend the scope of The Taoic totality itself. Buddhic Plane Entities are Physical Plane Time manipulators. They are the creators of species of living beings. They are in charge of the delineation of all Physical Plane energy. Buddhic Plane Entities are planet creators. They decide the workability of life species. They are matter manipulators. It is quite complex. They function outside of time. Or as we have stated in No-Time, such as we function. However, they are the creator-manipulators of Physical Plane Time in a linear sense.

Are there many other groups of Entities, similar to yourselves, who are also composite Entities?

Yes. There are many other groups of Entities functioning at different levels of Planes. These are composite Entities. There is however only one Fairns composite.

Is there a difference between The Fairns as a whole and The E'sef or The E'Fairn composite functioning alone?

The Fairns are The E'sef and E'Fairn composite Entities functioning together as one. We are different from other single composite Entities. We are using Fairns to mean both of our composite

Entities working together to make the Larger Entity.

You said that one Entity functions at the second level Mental Plane and the other Entity functions at seventh level Mental Plane. Those two levels of the Mental Plane are pretty far apart.
   Yes, It is necessary.

It must be that both parts of your unified Entity bring substantially different properties and characteristics if they are so far apart level wise.
   Correct. The E'Fairn part of our Rate, you might say, bleeds through to the Buddhic plane. That is why we are able to give concepts in larger aspects regarding those things which you study and then translate those concepts into words which are marginally workable.[4] You might say that the E'sef aspect of our being is our verbal translator. Is this understandable?

Yes, the E'sef aspect is your second level Entity.
   Correct.

If it were possible for us to perceive you, what would we perceive?
   It is a feeling of Fourth of July fireworks. There is also music. There is also much movement like wind funnels, you say tornados. There is action. It is not translatable. You could envision this: A white tornado with colored sparks flying around, through, and from it and of course sound - music, wonderful whirling music.

Which notes of music?
   All notes within your comprehension and many, many more.

Let's consider some of the practical aspects regarding your capabilities. You said that your system of making measurements and observations is different than ours.
   Correct.

How do you make observations?
   There are many ways for us to do this. It depends greatly upon

---

[4]This refers to discussions of the geometric basis of particle field theories.

the type of observation being requested.   Sometimes it is a thing which can be translated into numbers or quantities which include numbers.   At other times our observations are qualitative.   At times we make observations which function in what you call Simultaneity.   In other words, we can observe wholes, the whole of the action, while it is functioning.   It is difficult to measure a function while it is on going.   It is possible to observe and report instant to instant, but it is not always possible to define a constantly changing process, and thereby measure it.   For you who must attempt comprehension from a linear point of view, this may seem somewhat confusing.

Perhaps some specific examples would be helpful. We asked about the oxygen content of the atmosphere, the global percentage average over some period of time. How did you come up with that?

We made measurement requests from level two E'sef function observers.

Then they gave you the information.

It is like gearing down and finding the correct terms to measure the observation using your measurement terminology.   Then we report that measurement according to that specific instant within the ongoing process.

Sometimes you seem to struggle with numbers.

At times it can be more difficult because we see and read human Soul Patterns much more easily than what you call inert Physical matter.   Then there are struggles to translate correct numerical measurements using words within your understanding.   This is what causes us those difficulties along with the complexities of Simultaneous Time.   It is much easier to focus on a Soul Pattern through which we can read a given area.   If there is a person in the area to be read or measured then we can read that area more clearly.

You deal much better with living composite organisms like human beings. So if there is a person where you are looking then you can somehow read it easier. It is like shining a light on an area.

We can read the inert energies surrounding that human being, yes.

Under what restrictions do you operate with regards to the information you give us?

The main restriction is non-interference in terms of decision making or choices of those still functioning within the Physical Plane as individual Soul Patterns. The problem or risk is that if we state that a given thing "will" occur, our Rate of function, or our power you might say, makes that statement a reality that nothing can change. Therefore, when speaking of future time frames, if we stated "In X amount of time a thing will occur", stating that makes it an unchangeable reality. This is not allowed. We are violating our own Will directive and Taoic Will if we do that. We are allowed leeway in certain situations, however. The quantity of leeway varies subject to subject, person to person, topic to topic. It is difficult to make categorical statements regarding time frames. You have experienced times when we have stated "you will find" or "you will accomplish." In these instances we are able to make these statements if the individuals' choices have already been made.

You speak through Jasmine. How does her knowledge enter into the communication?

We have subtlety, with great care, encouraged Jasmine to investigate as many varied sources of information as possible. Of course, there is a certain limitation working through a Physical form. There is only a limited amount of information capable of being banked in the cellular structure you call the brain. Because a brain is a Physical Plane organ made of matter it must be accessed linearly. If we were to trigger a total access it could explode the organ itself. We must also use the vocabulary available within Jasmine. At times, at rare times, it is possible to access terms from those who are in very close proximity to Jasmine while we are speaking. We must however take great care when doing this for there is a certain body Rate adjustment that must occur for us to function through and this can be tricky. It is not our intention or wish to cause Physical damage. There are limitations when working through a Physical House. Jasmine's easy adjustment, quick adjustment in Rate, the very voluntary blankness achieved in such a short time makes the exchanges more clear and less influenced. When the vehicle does not resist the exchange mentally or emotionally, the clarity of the information given is greater.[5]

If Jasmine understood mathematics, say calculus, could you then

---

[5]Channels can become involved and add to the messages. When this happens the message becomes a composite creation.

accurately communicate to us using that knowledge?

It is more simply a lack of vocabulary which causes problems. However, some exposure would not be harmful.

You originally contacted Jasmine through a Ouija board. What is the significance of a Ouija board?

It was simply a training tool to build Jasmine's belief and confidence in shiself and what was already being heard in shis own mind. We sent our request through a Causal Plane Entity who then guided the message via a Ouija board. We mean the message concerning our request for contact be received by two persons who were in close Physical proximity to Jasmine. And the only way this message could be sent was because those two persons were experimenting with a Ouija board. Now we wish to put a small amount of humor, or you say tongue in cheek, and state that of course it is not the board that has any power at all. It is simply that those who sit and calm themselves with the ritual required to work a Ouija board place themselves in a mental vibrational Rate of consciousness where messages can be sent and received with much greater success. This phenomena is of course attributed to the Ouija board. Some think the board has "strange" power. However, it is only the workers state of consciousness when they sit down to a Ouija board. The tendency, of course, is much greater in your society to believe that an object outside of yourselves has power, believability, or credibility. You tend to assign what is heard or received from within as flights of imagination. When the message was sent had these two persons heard it in their minds, only, they would not have bothered to give it credence or pass it on. So the Ouija board served its purpose by spelling out our request and the request was relayed to Jasmine.

A Ouija board is similar to a crystal, then?

It is similar, but not the same. A Ouija board is not an enhancer. It is only an accepted tool to achieve a certain vibrational state of consciousness. Whereas the use of a crystal augments the intent of a person's thought after the vibrational state has been attained. Therefore crystals are much more directly effective and powerful in augmenting thought energies and intentions.

Can you read our minds or conscious thoughts?

We can read those thought feelings, yes. We have the ability to read minds. Whether or not we choose to state what is felt is another matter. We do not pry. To reveal what we see you think, whether or not you request this, would in many instances be a form of interference. It would be dishonoring of your personhood and an intrusion.

Can you read a book?
This is such a large giggle. If you open and refer to a book while Jasmine is out, you say, then we can, Yes. We do not read verbatim. However, we can read the intent and the content of the whole.

Do you use energy produced by humans?
The energy that you create gives us the means to communicate back, you might say. Yes.

Do you understand different languages? If I spoke in a language that Jasmine does not understand, say Russian, would you understand that?
Jasmine has had little exposure to that language. That is where the limitations come in. Jasmine needs to know the language.

You stated once that you were scanning all available photographs of the moon for a particular structure.
Correct.

How did you do that? Did you pass that request down, or did you do that yourself?
We were reading the Soul Patterns of the astronauts who had taken the photographs and experienced the evidence. Also, there are those Others, those People in-coming, who have an observation base on the dark side of the moon. They are on the moon much of the time working in shifts in the observation base. We can take readings through them.

Your frequency Rate is much faster than ours I assume, is that correct?
When attempting to translate our Rate into your terms of measurement the only effective way to state our Rate would be to use the concept of "Speed." Yes, our Rate/Speed is much faster.

Do you have a memory?
All that has ever happened, all that will ever happen, all the lives you have lived or will ever live you are living Now. All occurs

Now. Therefore the answer is yes and no. For though in your terms there is memory and we can have that, the fact that all is occurring Now means that we do not have to have memory for all is available for observation Now. It is a difficult concept: **Simultaneity.**

Yes, that gets into "time" and cause and effect. We have a special perception of that aspect of reality, by choice I assume.
    And by design. This is important. The Physical Plane - wherein the concept and the actuality of Time exists - is the only Rate at which energy can be created. Therefore, the Physical Plane and its function in linear time is absolutely essential. That is where energy - material, matter, energy - is made.

You mentioned earlier you use energy which we create. Is there a direct physical, emotional, or spiritual energy transfer from us to you?
    We do not directly tap an individual's personal energy, no. But humans as a whole are creating sustenance energy collectively in the Physical Plane. That energy expands and permeates outward to sustain all other Planes.

How does your data processing capability work? Does it work like a computer? How do you assess information or manipulate it?
    This depends upon what is requested.

To go back to a specific example, when you gave the average oxygen content of the atmosphere over one hundred years. That is a tremendous amount of data. There is time involved, all different places and different events, perhaps billions of pieces of data, and to be reduced to a single numerical result....
    We have what you call instant replay. You state a desired linear time frame cumulative observation. We make the most accurate approximate time measure possible using our Rate of measure, observe that, or re-observe (past), or pre-observe (future) the function within that requested time frame and give the conversion as you asked; an average percentage. It is possible to do that at times quite rapidly. So yes, it is like a huge computer function, but it is more similar to being there - an instantaneous cumulative observation made from the experiencing of the requested time frame.

What is your accuracy rate? What percentage of the material you

send gets through the translation process?

We are quite pleased to answer this question. Other than our glitches with numbers and linear time periods, which in our reality do not exist, we would state that in our observation of what is in print according to what we have wanted to express ninety seven percent accuracy is achieved.

Do you have physical location?

Yes, you can reach out your arms and they will be extended right through where we **Be**.

Space? Do you mean all of space or this little region where we are sitting?

We function in the same place as you function. It is simply a different Rate of function not place of function. Therefore you would say, yes, all of space.

Do you have a purpose or task that relates to humans?

You "Searchers" are our work. It is essential to never allow Physical Plane functioners to become desolate. In other words, it is essential for people to believe that they have a connection, a working relationship with all other Entities and Planes. Therefore, when there is great desperation, crisis, and potential, we work with those "Searchers" that remember within themselves: There is a connection; there is a larger Whole. Then the interaction between all Planes is reaffirmed and the circulation of the energy within The Whole of Whole is assured.

Do you have feelings? Can you feel happiness?

We can, with care, state yes. We can feel many different intensities. We often explain these variations (feelings) using the terms warm or coolness, slow or fastness. We do not experience what you would call Negative emotions. We do, however, have large fatness of feeling for Love and Joy. Although at times we have, through Jasmine, and through observations of certain deeds which people perpetrate upon each other, felt what you would call incensed sensations, hot we would say. It is not the people that are the cause however, it is the deed that causes us some intenseness.

Tao Song.

THE STRUCTURE OF THE GREATER REALITY

What does "Tao Song" mean?
ALL THAT IS is one - The singing of the Tao. What better greeting?

Do we have only one life on Earth?
The assumption that ALL THAT IS, The Tao, would expend such vast energy in the creation of Souls vested in the Physical Plane (the material universe) and then allow them only one incarnation in the Physical world would be a gross error. The Tao manifests parts of itself as self-aware patterned energy - Souls, with free choice. Each Soul enters the Physical Plane as an individualized entity who incarnates and reincarnates in a physical form as it progresses and refines its own creative energy. All energy in the Physical world is constantly re-cycled (birth-death-birth) so it can be re-shaped, re-formed into an ever-changing variety. Un-enSouled species have no conscious awareness of the circle of Physical creation, but when Souls entered Enedswr[6] bodies they brought conscious awareness. This made the House-Self[7] aware of the termination (death) of its individual House. This awareness, coupled with the strong survival drive of the species instilled the fear of "death". One of the greatest challenges of embodied Souls is to lead its House-Self to a conscious understanding that all is living creation, creative energy, that "death" is always a beginning again and again and again.

We can give this in linear terms, cautioning, however, that this is very precarious and simplified. The Tao created Souls, endowing these Souls with choice and free will and the power of creativity. By creating, they furnish eternal creative energy for The Tao itself. This is what is meant by "vested". One law of physics states a body in motion tends to stay in motion. One life and the concept of "death" is stasis. There is no static quality in any part or particle of the Universe, or The ALL THAT IS. There never has been any stasis. To provide energy for

---

[6]Enedswr (en-ed-ez-ware) - human being or any species which is conscious of self; any species with a soul.

[7]House-self - animal body instincts, house-body.

all that is, for The ALL THAT IS to **Be**, there must be and is perpetual motion. We state this to those of Western Civilization, in specific, the now Judeo-Christian: There can be no death and in the confines of the Physical Plane, there is reincarnation. Only one life would be void, nothingness, non. It is fortunate that many more Enedswr believe in the reality, the truth of reincarnation.

You speak of The Tao creating Souls and using Soul created Positive Energy to perpetuate itself. What is The Tao?

Taking into consideration the fact that only The Tao has complete comprehension and understanding of itself, we will state, from our understanding, it is the infinite, ever-expanding, Whole - The ALL THAT IS, in and out of the Physical Plane. The Tao is The ALL THAT IS, the Whole of the Whole Ad Infinitum.

Should we perceive The Tao as a personal god who oversees and controls the Physical Universe?

This concept is an exceedingly popular pastime in Western Culture. We state that this concept is not wrong, neither is it Negative. It is, however, very narrow, limited and entrapping of those who embrace it. It is much more effective and powerful in the creative sense to conceive of The Tao as a vast energy source from which it is possible to draw or focus energy in the form of guidance, or enlightenment, of comfort to each individual seeking this within shiself[8]. This does not close one within a long dark hall. This concept allows for as much expansion and variation as walking out-of-doors in the sunlight. You see, neither condition is wrong or right, it is simply a matter of choice or preference. Which would you chose?

Are you stating that each of us chooses our own interpretation of The Tao?

It is the tendency of Enedswr to encompass in comprehensible terminology that which is inherently known to be larger than self. In keeping with this - yes, the image of The ALL THAT IS is created. In Western Culture, Enedswr have created "God" and given "Him" a man's likeness.

Why isn't reincarnation a belief in Western Culture? If souls are

---

[8]Shis - she/he, his/her. The Fairns make no gender distinction.

aware of reincarnation then why is there not an innate conscious awareness of incarnation?

This is an exceedingly complex question. Basically, this is one of the great dichotomies of Physical Plane existence. The linear processes of the Physical Plane and its "life" are more blatantly obvious than the circular Whole. Enedswr also tend to attach and analyze isolated factors which makes corporeal life and death more important. We mean to say that the obviousness of a person's being born, growing old, and then passing becomes all conceivable. The body is the person; therefore, when the bodies dies, the person is no longer. It takes many lives in many bodies for the incarnate Soul to learn to remember its Soul-Self and its circular, as opposed to linear, existence. At times it is more comfortable and convenient to adhere to a totally linear concept of existence.

Why is linear thinking more convenient for Enedswr?

It explains the corporeal separateness and upholds what is sensually obvious. In other words, it provides a reason for separateness, individualness, one apart - the ultimate refinement of linear thinking. To embrace the circular, they lose that separateness, that house-satisfying individuality. When Enedswr become one with all, they can no longer adhere to divisiveness. Western Culture is imbued with individualness, the belief of "different from" - meaning better than all others. The philosophy that you shall be "whisked to the bosom of God" after one life is another means of stating the separateness from others and all. These points we have stated are only a few examples. To discuss the complete dichotomy, and Western Culture in specific, would be a great undertaking in itself. There is no pat answer for this. Many perpetuate the belief of separateness because it is accepted within the culture. However, this is rapidly changing. Reincarnation is becoming more realized world-wide.

Why do Souls incarnate in Physical bodies?

The creation of the Physical Plane, which encompasses all within the material Universe, is an expression of and a necessity for the functioning of The Tao itself. As there is and ever shall be The Tao, so there shall also be a Physical Plane or Universe. To function within the Physical Plane, Souls must choose a Physical body. On this Mother, you say planet, the choice is Enedswr. This choice is made for several physiological reasons - brain capacity, adaptability, manual dexterity. This land species (Homo Sapien) provides a superior choice.

When Souls are created, are they forced to incarnate and reincarnate in the Physical Plane?

Souls cannot initiate their own creative power unless they begin in the Physical Plane and because they are a part of the ever-creationing Tao, they seek the joy, sustenance and fulfillment of creating. This is what makes reincarnation a Law. The Tao is self-sustaining. Without reincarnation, there could be no sustenance for perpetual creation. Therefore, it is not force but choice.

Can you explain what that part of us is - Soul, psyche, spirit - that continues to live after the death of the Physical body?

When The Tao created Soul Patterns, each was engendered with awareness and the ability of cumulative retention. Remembrance not only of the individual pattern, but the potential experiences that Souls in Physical bodies could choose. On departing from the inhabited Physical body, this Soul Pattern, a part of The Whole of the Whole, is what "lives" and continues.

Do you mean that when a Soul is created, it is aware of all the possible Physical lives it may choose?

Souls are aware of their primary function, that is to create Positive energy for the Eternal Taoic Continuum. Also, they are aware of the means through which this function is achieved in the Physical Plane. All lives in the Physical are not predestined or pre-chosen. Different choices are made between incarnations, but the myriad possibilities of Physical life are known before the first incarnation.

Could you explain further "predestined or pre-chosen"?

We mean to state that, in your terms, before the primary incarnation, the particular choices and experiences of each life are not accomplished. But the possible combinations, possible experiences which are available in the Physical are known. It is something such as this: "I can do this, I can do that, this variation is possible with this embellishment here, etc". But the solidification of each life choice is not made before the primary incarnation. The complexities of coping with the House-Self, the House drives and needs are/were not available to the Souls. It is like preparing for a certain occupation and being exceedingly learned but having no experience. There is no substitute for experience. If the Soul-Self, upon entering the House, remained in total and absolute control of all House actions, there would be no necessity for the Physical Plane. To initiate or to activate, each Soul's power of

"To Creationing" of energy for use by The Tao, the Physical body must be entered. This is the switch, so to speak, which turns on the power. Physical embodiment initiates the beginning of creativity between the Soul and House-Self. This causes the seeming dichotomy of the struggle to learn, to coordinate, and harmonize within one the function of both for the Positive sustenance of The Tao. This seeming struggle, the attempt toward harmony is why there is progression through reincarnation. It is a Positive, on-going attempted resolution of function between Soul-Self and House-Self which is culminated when in the last lifetimes, the House and Soul are one. Then the Soul need no longer reincarnate in the Physical Plane. It is then prepared to continue its "To Creationing" off or out of the Physical Plane - that which you call Spiritual Plane.

What do you mean different choices are made between our Physical lives and what are these choices?

Choices made between Physical lives are decided upon by each Soul in an attempt to gain the most learning and knowledge geared towards harmonic functioning of Soul-in-House. Each Soul chooses those situations which excel toward the most effective creation of Positive in the overall Taoic function of The ALL THAT IS. The Soul chooses its geographic location, its parentage, sex, and material situation; also the quality and condition of the specific body, its physical function, looks and "intelligence" potential. All these factors contribute to different learning, experience, and off-plane goals. For example, a Soul might choose to work towards harmony under the conditions of poverty and deprivation. Another might choose to attempt harmony and acquire altruism in conditions of opulence. All these and even finer details can be pre-incarnation choices. But remember, all is choice, and all Souls, while incarnate, are free to change the scripts of their plays, to ad lib, so to speak, and they often do.

When does the Soul enter a new body it has chosen for an incarnation?

When a new House is conceived whose circumstances fulfill the choices of the Between Soul, the Soul then guides and hovers about the House until, and in some circumstances, for a short period of your time after the moment of birth. The Soul does not enter the House prior to the moment of birth and can and often does deliberate the choice for as long as two weeks to a month afterward. The available conclusions and ramifications you can draw from this are obvious. If there is no Soul desiring the particular new House, and therefore, neither hovering or entering upon the moment of birth, the new House will "die" and its energy will be recycled. The continued life of the new House depends upon whether or not a Soul decides to solidify its choice and enter. Failure of the Soul to solidify its off-plane choice results in Sudden Infant Death Syndrome.

Do Souls choose the length of each lifetime and the way they will end it?

This question is more complicated than it seems. We will say yes, it is chosen. However, it is not a solidified between incarnation choice, although under certain circumstances, it can be. This choice is an on-going creation of each Soul during the specific incarnation. It can be a conscious creation of the Soul-in-House as it progresses through the specific lifetime. The Soul creates the physical condition of its House during the entire lifetime, choosing the periods of health or illness it desires to experience and ultimately choosing the means for terminating its stay in the House.   But once in the House, these choices are influenced by the needs and drives of the House-Self and the cultural beliefs with which it is imbued. As with all the specific circumstances a person experiences in each lifetime, the Soul-Self, always influenced by the House-Self, chooses and creates its incarnation "play"[9]. It can change any circumstance it no longer wishes to experience simply by changing its thoughts and beliefs.

Do you have any comments for the readers?

Within your comprehension, Creative Consciousness, Mind, Thought is of the totality of The Tao itself. Thought forms all Physical reality and creates all energy.   Thought is the source of all communication. Expressed in language, feelings, or pictures, it is the medium of communication of all Souls in all Planes with each other and with The Tao. Thoughts of Souls not incarnate on the Physical Plane can be received by incarnate Souls no matter what language is used in any Physical existence. We often send feelings, pictures, and diagrams along with specific terminology to express our meaning. Very often it is difficult to force concepts into words, Jasmine, one of the expressors of our thought in the Physical Plane, receives more of the gestalt meanings we send. To project this forth in language so that all may

---

[9]Play - life outline; life design or potential design

hear, we tend to over-exercise rhetoric. However, to over-use terms of language is less risky than to "slice" too "thin" and produce a narrow confining definition or statement. We have found that the exercise of wading through circular language is very beneficial to produce within the Searcher a more rounded technique in everyday thought. We will state here that it is very, very important to initiate circular thinking as opposed to linear thinking. We are as intense to experience the joyfulness of communication and teaching as all Searchers are to hear Truth and experience the joy of Truth. We say "menerk vo"[10] to all who read our teachings and "hear".

You stated that Souls enter bodies to create Positive Energy for the "To Creationing" of The Tao. How do ensouleds create energy?
        We say this: It is very simple, it is very complex, but easy to understand. The ensouled body is in essence a chemically charged, organically manifested, pattern of energy. In other words, the human brain, ensouled, is a battery which ends on the death of the hive House. While the hive body is ensouled, it is continually creating or producing energy. **All thought is newly created energy.**

Is energy created on Planes other than the Physical?
        It is dependant upon the Physical Plane to provide the Positive energy which makes communication and interaction between the Physical and the Non-Physical Planes possible.

If Souls know before they enter the Physical Plane they are to create "Positive", why do they create so much "Negative".
        This potential is a drawback of inhabiting an animal hive body. The great dichotomy of ensouling a hive body is the awareness of trying to consciously elevate the combination of Soul-in-House without isolating or separating that condition of being from the natural working of all that comprises the Physical and The ALL THAT IS - The Whole of Whole. This is the most difficult stage of existence , on or off the Physical Plane.

Why do Souls choose to be so powerless when they enter a hive House, adapting to the instincts of the House rather than the awareness of the Soul?

---

[10]Menerk Vo - Thank you very much in the Athlenta language.

It is this: In order for the Houses to have physical strength and adaptability and the innate "intelligence" able to support the actual physical drain of housing a Soul - an energy from another rate - the Houses had to have nearly ten times the survival drive instinct of other hive Houses. This "House-survival-will" is so strong that it acts as a neutralizer for the remembering of the Soul. When Souls first choose to experience the Physical they assisted the hive House species, Homo Sapien, to evolve to the point where they could sustain the inhabitation of the Soul Pattern. This, in terms of linear time is what you call the "dawn of man". The Soul must accept hive conditions in order to be Physical. Souls' desires to experience the Physical can be paralleled to physically bound Souls' desires to experience out-of-body existence beyond the Physical. The unembodied Souls' desires to reach "in" is as intense as embodied Souls' desires to reach "out". The ultimate "why" lies with the Infinite To Creationing - The Tao. In other words, all is given as it is given, all is answered as and when it is answered. For us, also, waiting is nice. Do you understand?

How are we, as humans, similar to the animal species?

The hive House of Homo Sapien Sapien is a hive animal species. Just as canines, or felines, or Cetacean House or body is a hive animal species. The key to understand is that the relative hive body, the ambulation, the skeletal, cranial, and the encephalic structure of the species Homo Sapien Sapien can sustain an individual Soul Pattern - can be ensouled. Where as the other hive animal bodies, or Houses, or species, other than Cetaceans, cannot sustain the individual Soul Pattern. It is important to understand that you in hive body is exactly that - you in the hive body. That which makes you eternal, You, can only be sustained on this Mother in the hive species Homo Sapien Sapien.

Must all Souls go through the Physical first before they can return to The Tao?

Souls experience some aspect of the Physical, yes. We say there are no limitations placed on Souls. Does The ALL THAT IS regulate itself? No. If the Physical Plane creates enough Positive for Balance and communication between Physical and Non-Physical, then there is no strain on the Stress Ether for function between the Physical and Non-Physical. When the majority of energy created on the Physical is Negative, there is an increasing drain upon the Stress Ether in order to bring messages through to the Physical Plane. We will give this picture: When Positive energy is not created in the Physical, to our

Planes, it is as though there were a door locked from your side and we can only shout through the peep hole to be heard. The creation and maintenance of Positive energy from the Physical unlocks this door and swings it wide so that the energy flows between the Planes.

What is the Stress Ether?

The easiest manner to describe the Stress Ether, and there is no simple concept of this, is that the Stress Ether is the medium in which all Patterns are carried, all energy flows, and all that is of The ALL THAT IS functions. It is possibly more clear to describe the Stress Ether as the blood of The Taoic Body. It is what you would call the "space" between things. It is most essential. It is the circulatory system that carries essential energy to all parts of The Taoic Body.

When we produce Positive energy, does it flow immediately to the Stress Ether where it is used as needed, either in the Physical or Non-Physical?

The energy that is not focused or directed, yes.

We are visualizing this body of Stress Ether as carrying directed energy and free flowing energy available for tapping. Are we accurate?

Yes. This is accurate, but only one condition or attribute of the Stress Ether is represented in your definition. We say that the all important factor to remember, the opposite of which is so deeply ingrained in this now, is that **it is a fact that energy is created.** There is not a static amount which is simply distributed and re-distributed, borrowed, returned, used or used up. A Soul, through desire and intent, can focus energy from the Stress Ether through the Soul-Self, but can also draw a small amount of Stress Ether energy to focus a larger amount of newly created thought energy which in turn is used and also replenishes that energy flicked from the Stress Ether itself.

If Souls on the Physical Plane are constantly creating new energy, why doesn't the amount of energy in the Physical Universe constantly increase?

We can give some concepts narrowed for comprehension and some aspects of Universal meaning - Taoic Laws, which can be applied. A complete wholistic aspect of Taoic function, we cannot give as we are not The ALL THAT IS.

The ALL THAT IS, the Whole of Whole, The Tao, is the process of creation, that is, To Creationing ad infinitum.
The ALL THAT IS and all that is part of The ALL THAT IS, is in a state of infinite expansion.

Think of the Physical Universe as being surrounded by a semi-permeable membrane through which only Positive energy may flow from either direction. Within the confines of the membrane there are not two types of energy working, but four.

1. Positive energy.
2. Negative energy.
3. The interaction of Positive and Negative, which gives Neutral.
4. Balanced to Positive or Activated Positive, which is immediately available for all Planes.

There is Positive energy being created which passes freely. The Negative energy being created does not pass freely.   There is the interaction of the two which is a Neutral form which passes freely. There is the creation of Balanced to Positive which passes immediately for use by other Planes. Positive energy is created by either thought or deed or manner of being which allows all other Enedswr, the Planet and shis children, and the Physical Universe to be complemented and not interfered with. Humans create Negative energy when the impetus for any action begins with premeditated divisiveness for the purposes of gain or aggrandizement. Any thought, decision, or action which divides creates Negative. The outcome of the interaction between Positive and Negative energies is Neutral energy. It is Positive in that it does not create or harbor Negative. In other words in is a Neutral form. It is a form which is non-interfering but at the same time un-usable. It does not create imbalance for the Physical Plane but it creates no usable Positive for the Non-physical Planes.

There is Balanced energy, which in actuality, is a **plus** Positive. It is an activated form of Positive energy which becomes immediately usable by Non-Physical Plane. It can be used by Non-Physical Plane for assistance of the Physical Plane, or in your terms, actively sent back. It can also be available energy for the necessary functioning and work of Non-Physical Planes. Balanced to Positive energy is when all aspects which went into the creation of that specific form of Positive energy

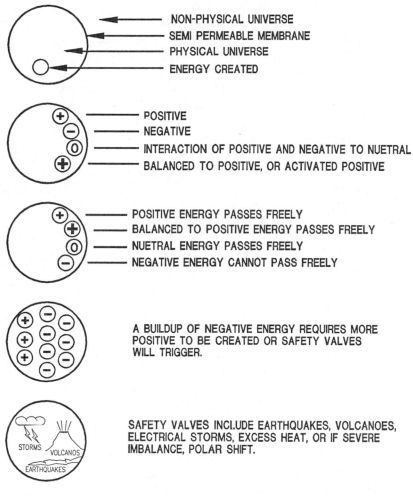

NON-PHYSICAL UNIVERSE
SEMI PERMEABLE MEMBRANE
PHYSICAL UNIVERSE
ENERGY CREATED

POSITIVE
NEGATIVE
INTERACTION OF POSITIVE AND NEGATIVE TO NUETRAL
BALANCED TO POSITIVE, OR ACTIVATED POSITIVE

POSITIVE ENERGY PASSES FREELY
BALANCED TO POSITIVE ENERGY PASSES FREELY
NUETRAL ENERGY PASSES FREELY
NEGATIVE ENERGY CANNOT PASS FREELY

A BUILDUP OF NEGATIVE ENERGY REQUIRES MORE
POSITIVE TO BE CREATED OR SAFETY VALVES
WILL TRIGGER.

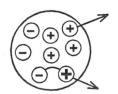

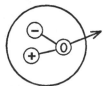

SAFETY VALVES INCLUDE EARTHQUAKES, VOLCANOES,
ELECTRICAL STORMS, EXCESS HEAT, OR IF SEVERE
IMBALANCE, POLAR SHIFT.

THE INTERACTION OF POSITIVE AND NEGATIVE ENERGY
TO A NUETRAL KIND PASSES FREELY. IT DOES NOT
BUILD UP, BUT IS NOT USABLE IN THE NON-PHYSICAL
PLANES.

EXCESS POSITIVE PASSES FREELY FOR USE BY
NON-PHYSICAL PLANES.

BALANCED TO POSITIVE ENERGY NUETRALIZES A
NEGATIVE AND STILL HAS POSITIVE LEFT OVER
WHICH PASSES IMMEDIATELY FOR USE BY
NON-PHYSICAL PLANES.

were Positive.   A thought is brought forth with Positive intent, the decision to take action upon that thought is based in Positive, and the subsequent action is carried forth in Positive.   That is what gives the Balanced to Positive its extra intensity.

Within the Physical Plane, which is surrounded by this membrane,   only a certain amount of energy is capable of being contained and still be that which it must be - **manifestation of matter.** Ensouled species within the Physical Plane are constantly creating new energy. We cannot explain this in words. It simply Is. Newly created additional energy moves to the Stress Ether and then out of the confines of the Physical Plane unless this energy is Negative. Negative energy cannot permeate the membrane. Therefore, there is a build up. As of this Now your science has no way to perceive or measure this when it occurs. The problem is that it is not a constant, or steady occurrence and, in your terms, happens so quickly that specialized methods and instruments of measure do not suffice in either time or place.

Now, within the Physical Universe there are planned safety valves engaged by the original Taoic play to equalize an excess of Negative energy. On this planet these safety valves are earthquakes, volcanic eruptions, severe storms, and intense heat and winds.   If Enedswr create a constant Balance of Negative and Positive, then the creation is Balanced Energy which leaves through the semi-permeable membrane by means of the Stress Ether. When plus Positive is created, this is activated, usable on all Planes, To Creationing, energy. **Balance in the Physical** is a constant state of stasis or existence and nothing more. The key to continuance in laughter is maintaining Balance in the Physical while at the same time creating a **plus** of Activated Positive energy which instantaneously passes through the membrane and is immediately available for To Creationing. Due to these conditions of Taoic design, it appears to Now science that energy is set, but such is not the case. **Energy is continually created by ensouled beings in the Physical Plane.**

Within the Pattern of each ensouled, there is a mechanism of alert which functions when an act is potentially a violation. In some, this is greatly muted. Those actions, intents or processes which carry neither hindrance nor detriment to the "natural workings" of the systems of the Planet or its living beings can be considered Positive. We say, that which is **Considered,** and from a wholistic viewpoint, is that which is Positive. For "Consideration," we define this term as <u>Beneficial</u>

Wholism Assessment[11] in terms of planet and shis living systems. If an intent or a process is initiated without **Consideration,** then this is "Negative." We do not mean to rein or harness any quest for knowledge, but knowledge can only be called that, if the Planet and shis living systems do not suffer for that search.

Are you saying that "knowledge" gained by violating the planet or its living systems is inaccurate or not a true description of "reality"?
      The most effective term for these pieces which are found or thought is **factual sterility.** Does one travel a path and rejoice when the culmination of that path is a wall? Those items of information which cannot be Considerately applied to the Beneficially Assessed functioning of the living Planet and shis children are worth less than nothing. There is no such process as the favorite doctrine or motto of the so-called scientist: "Knowledge for knowledge's sake." For any thought, discovery, or process to be knowledge, it must be **an applied Beneficial Assessment.** It must be a functioning in **Consideration** of the Mother and those who live thereon. All else is factual sterility, nil-non-absence. This is, as you have unraveled, a **Taoic Primary Law.** Translated in linear words, it is this: **Knowledge is the functioning Beneficial Assessment encompassing the guidelines for and within the Plane in which this knowledge seeks to become.**
      The Physical Plane exists within its framework of functioning according to Taoic Laws. **Any Beneficial Assessment in keeping with this framework and the ensouleds' home within this framework is knowledge.** This holds true for all Planes. Each functions within its framework according to Taoic Law. Discoveries in any Plane framework that are Considerate of that framework are knowledge. It is not Beneficial Assessment of the framework itself, it is Beneficial Assessment of the knowledge in keeping with The Taoic framework. The functioning must be harmonicly Balanced within the framework which makes each Plane specific to itself.

You have stated that all is Energy. We are still trying to understand the difference between Energy in the Physical and Energy in other Planes.
      All is **Mind** energy. Energy as you define and understand the

----

[11]See also Chapter Fourteen for a discussion of Beneficial Wholism Assessment.

term in the Physical Plane is the Physical structure of <u>Mind</u> or <u>Thought</u> Energy. Thought Energy is the same in all Planes. Souls **Are** and **Use** Thought Energy. Souls are Patterned Thought Energy who think. Thought Energy can manipulate, create or control all other forms of energy in the Physical Plane. The Soul brings to the brain the ability to create, use, and interpret Thought Energy. You must realize that when bound to the Physical Plane, it is not possible to perceive any form of energy. It is only possible to perceive the results of energy. Scientists in this Now are not even willing to acknowledge the results of Thought Energy. How can they possibly acknowledge that **thought is energy**? It is ironic that they do not realize all questions, ideas, study, and investigations as to the "nature of the Universe" are a result of Thought Energy, the energy that creates the Physical Plane. It has been stated succinctly by a Soul incarnate, "I think, therefore, I am." So it is on all Planes.

You have told us you are on the Mental Plane. How many Planes are there?

We have stated that we **be** in or on the Mental Plane. There are seven Planes of **being** in which Patterned energy exists as units. The Tao is not a Plane or a Patterned unit. The Tao encompasses all Planes, but is also greater than, or more than, all Planes. It is ALL THAT IS and also <u>Itself.</u> Many different terms are used for naming the Planes of **being**. This is not really important. However, if giving names helps clarify or solidify this concept in your minds, we can give a list.

Physical: First is the Physical Plane, which, like all other Planes, exists according to a specific Taoic structure devised to sustain and order that part of the Whole. This Plane is Physical by nature of these Taoic Laws of structure, function, and order. For a "thing" to be Physical, it must be of the specific properties of energy which manifest material aspects - matter perceivable by beings consisting of matter who/which operate within The Taoic structure and Laws devised for the Physical Plane. This is very risky as it seems to be saying that something does not exist, if it cannot be seen, heard, felt, etc., and we do assure you that there are aspects of the Physical Plane which are confounding to your "Now" means of sensual perception. However, the Physical Plane is manifestation of energy as matter perceivable by beings of matter.

Astral: The Astral Plane is the second Plane and consist of three levels: lower, middle, and upper. These may be given individual names, but they are retained more easily when termed in this manner.

The Astral Plane is the main source of tangible contact with the Physical Plane. Although many do not recognize this fact, nearly all Enedswr can "project," and have "projected," their Souls into the Astral Plane during the sleep state. This occurs in the Middle Astral.

How and why does a Soul return to the Astral Plane during sleep?

During the state of "deep sleep," a Soul can leave the body on "hold," so to speak, and return to Astral Plane for counsel, guidance, or inspiration. Often when confronted with a difficult choice or with an "idea" it cannot formulate while in-House it will return to the Astral Plane for an off-Plane perspective. When you have a problem or are "out of sorts" with one of your fellow Enedswr, are you not advised to "sleep on it"?

The Lower Astral is reserved for Souls who have recently passed from the Physical Plane and must experience adjustment to Non-Physical existence according to creations which have been brought about by beliefs adhered to in the Physical Plane. Beliefs about the "hereafter" are enacted and experienced during the period of adjustment and this occurs in the Lower Astral. The upper Astral Plane is for counseling and preparation by Souls between lives for their return to the Physical Plane.

Mental and Causal: The fifth Plane is the Causal. The sixth Plane is the Mental. Much of the work of the Causal Plane is providing counsel for Souls in the upper Astral and helping them coordinate their return to the Physical. As one moves among the more intense Rates of the upper Causal and Mental Planes, it becomes more and more difficult to give a description that is comprehensible in Physical terms. It is easier to give a description of the work being done than to confine by definition the function of those Entities within these Planes. The upper Causal and Mental Planes are for philosophical assessment and teaching.

Buddhic: The Buddhic Plane Entities have the joy and responsibility of effecting energy into matter. Living forms on the Physical Plane are their **creationing.** It is difficult to make this felt correctly. In linear terms, one might say that plant and animal essences are governed, created, distributed, and reassessed for recyclement by Buddhic Plane Entities. After a Soul chooses a body in which to reincarnate and enters that body, it then determines the further creation of its house in accordance with the **Maya beliefs** it accepts while on the Physical, and also according to pre-life choices and needs for growth

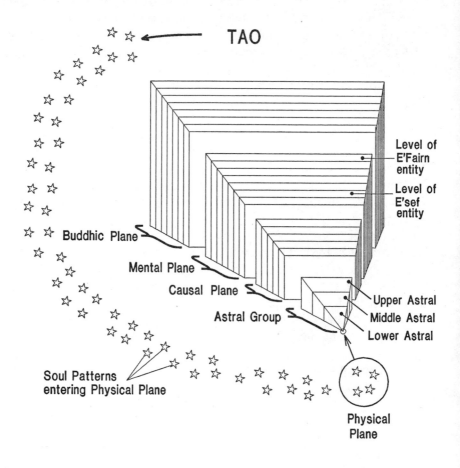

Pyramid Representation of the Greater Reality

performance within that body[12].   So with potentially ensouled hive species, the Buddhic Plane Entities allow greater fluidity concerning the the development of the specific form of the house.   But when the Soul passes, the Buddhic Entities govern recyclement of the body energy according to the function of Taoic Law in the Physical Plane.

It is important to understand that the levels of the Non-Physical Planes are not as evidently divided as the level from Physical Plane to Non-Physical Planes.   That is the greatest division: Physical to Non-Physical.

Is it safe to say the Soul experiences all lifetimes at once? Although we are only in a Physical body for a period of linear time?

What an astutely felt observation; taking into consideration that you are assessing this from a linear perspective. With that in mind, with great care, we would state yes, you are correct.

Then if we can access past lives, we can access future lives.

This is also correct. However, because of the necessity of the Physical House to process information linearly; because the body cannot sustain the entirety without burning up; we are not allowed to speculate on what you comprehend as your "future lives."   These you must process or access for yourselves. It is not a risk to your own body or brain to develop that ability for yourself.   It is, however, highly physically dangerous for us to open or reveal this for you.

When we dream or have out-of-body experiences, we sometimes move out into the Astral Plane and out of the Physical Plane?

Correct. During the sleep state a Soul can leave the body on "hold" and return to the Astral Plane for guidance or inspiration from a Backer.

Do we ever move from the Physical Plane to the Causal Plane and back, or Mental Plane?

No.   The Astral Plane first and second levels is used, or reserved for, or functions for those who are still in the process of experiencing Physical lives. Upper level: third level Astral Plane is where most, not all, but most Backers, or Guides reside. There is easy

---

[12]Maya - Illusion; social acculturation and/or indoctrination; handed down belief systems.

function, exchange between third level Astral and Causal Plane Entities. Seth is a Causal Plane Entity[13]. Between incarnations, all Souls abide in the Astral Plane. Astral Plane is a Rate where Soul Patterns function between Physical Plane incarnations. Once a Soul quits the Astral Plane, or moves out of the Astral, they no longer reincarnate at all.

How do the Soul Patterns move into the Causal Plane or the Mental Plane?

Souls change Planes when the work of that level is finished. Then the Rate is increased and Entities continue expansion and continue to - how would you say, enlarge - to reunite with other Soul Patterns of their accumulating Entity. There are functioning single composite Entities which have as many as three hundred thousand individual Soul Patterns. These are Composite Buddhic Plane Entities.

How many Buddhic Plane Entities are there? I think you mentioned three or four so far.

We are able to communicate, make requests, and receive information from three Buddhic Entities, Yes. If you are thinking of size, you could use Jasmine's crystal pyramid [14]as an example of how to imagine the scope, the expansion, and the numbers of Entities as they expand through the Planes. It is necessary to turn the pyramid upside down and think of the tip as Physical Plane. As the progressions through the Planes are accomplished everything gets fat fast. Of course it is much more like a sphere. Think of starting with a balloon which inflates as you blow air into it.

What is the difference between the way Patterned Energy - Souls - manifest on each of the Planes?

This is nearly impossible to describe. We will attempt a correlation. It is similar to the different peoples of Enedswr on your Mother. There is the ability for Non-Physical Entities to recognize other Entities from the various Planes. The inter-action between the upper Astral, the Causal and Mental Planes is more frequent than between those Planes and the Buddhic Plane. The upper levels of the Mental Plane can send a request for communication with those Entities

---

[13]Seth is the Entity who spoke through Jane Roberts.

[14]See figure on page 30.

comprising the Buddhic Plane, but the occasions arise very infrequently. Not only are Non-Physical Entities capable of distinguishing the differences of Plane, but the type of study and work of the Entities is also immediately recognizable. It would be similar to stating that all of one level are doctors, another are musicians, another philosophers, etc.

Can you explain the philosophical assessment and teachings of the Upper Causal and Mental Planes?

It is study of function of Taoic Law, learning that which is available to function within that Plane. Assisting the lower Planes to more clearly accomplish knowledge of Truth function of their Planes and also that which can be understood of The Taoic Truth.

Could you use yourselves as an example of what you mean?

You are our work. That action taking place at this Now is our work. There is also much study and learning, preparation and study of the infinite intricacies of Balance in the Physical and Non-Physical states concerning function of energy and **being**; The Balance of function of **Mind.** The Buddhic Plane then takes this knowledge and experiments or creates Physical beings. They get to "Creation" their learnings of function. We on the Mental learn and teach ingredients. Buddhic Entities "Make the Bread," so-to-speak. We teach to all who will open to hear according to each one's ability to comprehend. These teachings will be in accord with the levels of comprehension for each Plane.

What do you mean when you say that in the Lower Astral Plane Souls experience the beliefs they have adhered to during their last incarnation on the Physical Plane?

We wish to restate that **beliefs create reality.** If an Enedswr believes there is a "place" in the "hereafter" where rewards or punishments are meted out in accordance with shis behavior during that "lifetime," then after passing from the Physical, the period of adjustment to Non-Physical existence will incorporate the reality of those beliefs and the Soul will experience the condition according to shis own assessment of self. The lower Astral Plane is the "where" in which these belief creations are experienced. But ultimately, Souls are guided to understand that "the heaven or hell" they are creating for themselves are figments of beliefs carried "across" from the Physical Plane and are not reality in the sense of reality functioning of Taoic Law. These Souls are then re-introduced to the reality function of the **reason for being** and are assisted to the Middle Astral Plane. Here creative assessment of the previous life can be made without the influence of residual Maya, and preparations for another incarnation can be made.

Does the Soul itself choose which level of the Astral Plane it enters when it passes from the Physical Plane, or do Souls on other Planes make this determination?

No one Soul may make decisions for another. All are provided with guidance and information that assists the Soul in making decisions for itself. We see if you re-examine the truth that you **create your own reality,** many of these incongruencies will clarify. The Astral Plane is the most difficult to understand because fluidity is necessary for its function. There are divisions, but they are not as defined as the divisions between the other Planes and are nothing like your concept of division which is **bi-polar.** You only have two things to compare: Physical consciousness and dreams; Physical existence and Non-Physical existence. Thus division as defined on the Physical is different from the fluid separations of the Astral Plane.

Where do the other Planes exist in relation to our Physical Universe?

Speaking in terms of Taoic Reality, there is no actual division of any part of The Whole. All Planes exist and function with equal dispersion among ALL THAT IS. All Planes function within, around, and through The Taoic Whole. This is difficult to comprehend as, spatially speaking, there are no divided areas containing one Plane or another. Because you understand only linear and spatial relations while on the Physical Plane, and your language is so structured, our explanations may make it seem as though there are defined "areas" for each Plane. But such is not the case. You are not "there" and we "here." All Planes commingle.

If a Soul does not wish to return to the Physical Plane, must it do so?

Every Soul's inherent knowing and drive is to complete itself in **Oneness.** It may be said that the only way **out,** you say, is **through.** Only when the Soul is in a House where different cultural stresses, indoctrination, and especially Maya overshadow the Soul-Self does this conflict and anxiety arise; that is, the desire to be finished and quit this "veil of tears." When the Soul is at the rest and assessment period between lives, there is no conflicting anxiety concerning this progression through to **Oneness** with The ALL THAT IS.

Will you explain what you mean by Maya?

Maya, giving the Eastern philosophical definition, is that of Illusion. In more comprehensible terms here, we mean it to be interpreted as the accepted laws, mores, and values of society which, of course, are different in many areas or countries. Maya is the accumulated, handed-down acculturation and indoctrination which can and does veil the voice of the Soul-Self and control the "truths" with which one creates ones own reality. It is the belief structure that establishes the rules and regulations of the society within which an ensouled Enedswr functions.

Can a person's belief system influence Taoic Laws?

Excellent question. The Maya beliefs or any beliefs do not change the immutable Taoic Laws. They only affect your perceptions of those Laws - your ability to perceive those Laws. It is Taoic Law that Enedswr create their own reality, and the energy and ability to create whatever reality they believe in is available and possible. However, if Enedswr **create the reality** , that they do <u>not</u> create their own reality, this still does not change The Taoic Law that **Enedswr create their own reality**. As a Soul progresses through the Physical Plane and develops a stronger control over the House-Self, shis begins to question the "rightness" of the reality shis creates according to shis Maya beliefs, and the Soul-Voice sparks the drive of the "Searcher" to find The Taoic Reality, to understand The Taoic Laws which bring all into Balance and Oneness with The ALL THAT IS -The Tao.

Do individual or group beliefs operate only on the Physical Plane or are Souls' creations on other Planes influenced by their belief systems?

As Souls progress though the Non-Physical Planes, they acquire a broader and broader comprehension of the scope, purpose and function of Taoic Laws. The Physical Plane is the only Plane in which belief systems can and do create mistaken or counter-productive interpretations of Taoic Laws. Souls off the Physical Plane still may have limited comprehension of the totality of Taoic Law, but there is no possibility of their functioning belief systems being in opposition to the Law of Balance - a **plus** of Positive Energy. Souls in other Planes perpetuate **only** Positive Energy.

How and when does a Soul decide it no longer needs to reincarnate on the Physical Plane?

When all possible Positive experiences are accomplished and all Karma is clear, the Soul knows it need no longer incarnate on the Physical Plane. When all Taoic Laws governing the function of the Physical Plane are experienced in Positive and Balance, a Soul is **through** the Plane.

What do you mean by Karma?

There are many definitions of this term and those who adhere to a belief system based upon a certain definition give to the reality of Karma varying results according to their own belief system. We tend to proscribe to less vindictive or burdensome definition of Karma. We do not consider Karma predestined or immutable. There is a splendidly accurate definition of Karma already spoken: **"What ye sow, so shall ye reap."**

A list of actions which create Karma gives a clearer understanding than a definition of the word itself. The most blatant creation of Karmic nature comes through violence; through planned, deliberate actions intended to do harm to or interfere with any ensouled life. There is also a degree of Karma which can be accrued if an Enedswr seeks deliberately to perpetrate mass destruction of any living system or hive. Premeditated violence creates Karma. Premeditated war and Physical assault of any nature or outcome are the greatest incurrers of Karma. But remember, Karmic acts do not blemish or pollute the Soul in any way. They simply must be Balanced. Incurred Karma is Balanced over many lifetimes, and the Soul owed a Karmic debt may choose how and in what lifetime it will be Balanced.

There is also Positive Karma. Individual Souls and groups of Souls who share a loving, harmonious relationship in one lifetime may receive the Karmic Boon of sharing a harmonic relationship in another lifetime.

Belief in Karma may cause some Enedswr to create feelings of anxiety over "having to return many times" to the Physical Plane. But off-plane, all Souls know that regardless of any violent Karmic acts perpetrated while on the Physical, no Soul is lost, all Souls progress to become **One**. All that is **is** The ALL THAT IS. The Tao never wastes or loses any part of itself.

In linear terms, how often does a Soul reincarnate on the Physical Plane?

Young Souls tend to reincarnate much more often and more quickly than Mature and Older Souls. As a Soul progresses in its lessons through the Physical Plane, more "time" is taken between Physical lives for assessment and planning. Some older Souls may stay off the Physical Plane for as long as five hundred to a thousand years between lives. Very young Souls may reincarnate as quickly as one generation. All these returns depend upon the choices of the between-life Soul.

How many times does a Soul reincarnate in the Physical Plane?

The number of times depends upon the Soul growth during each lifetime and Karmic Balance. When an in-House Soul remembers that All Is One, that All is Balance, and lives in harmony with all Physical creation, loving without expectation; and when a Soul's Karmic debts are canceled, it no longer reincarnates in the Physical Plane if it chooses not to do so.

You have referred to young, mature, and old Souls. What do you mean by this?

In the fragmented beginning, when a part of MIND leaves The Tao to circle through the Planes to the Unified End, it assumes conscious awareness of itself and agrees to follow the developmental stages of the Physical House in which it incarnates. Through many "lifetimes" it "grows" in experience and in its ability to remember its source and its purpose, just as a Physical body grows from infancy to old age.

Is it accurate to say then that if one has an Astral Plane experience, basically, they move into a situation where time stops?

If it is middle Astral Plane,- Yes, time stops. This is quite tricky to understand because the perception of time does not stop. Time and perception of time can be experienced in different ways.

What about the problem of how we comprehend time? If, in the future, we will evolve into a Casual Plane entity, a Mental Plane Entity, etc. does that not mean there is an existing extension of myself already - that you can observe and interact with - or am I misunderstanding the physics.

It is possible for us to read this higher extension of yourself yes, but it is not allowed while your consciousness experiences only your singularity, your aloneness, your individuality. If we read and delineate "No-time" to you as an individual, functioning in linear time, we would be violating Taoic Universal Function which is based on Simultaneity -

or you say, free choice.   You   cannot conceive, see yourself, or experience your other "No-times" of self simultaneously. The Physical brain can not process all experience simultaneously. Therefore, it is necessary to do the same thing with Physical Plane time that we spoke of with spinors[15]. The points can be stretched in any direction. This is one function which Buddhic Plane Entities accomplish: the malleability potentials of Time; the continuity aspects of material and non-material energies. The Buddhic Plane designs all Physical Plane species and all potential species, along with all forms of material energy such as rocks etc. including the linear time in which they "be."

Trying to understand time completely is like beating our heads against the wall.

Maybe all walls in all times. But, please do not hurt your heads. There is only one time within the greater reality of The Whole of the Whole. We call this "No-Time."

The problem is we can not see it.

You can see it when you be it. We mean when you experience it, yes. But Physical Plane time is the embodiment of linear function. When you experience what you call out of body; that is relatively similar to "No-Time."

We have a concept of Physical Law, like laws of gravity, laws of force. We know these are not entirely correct or complete, but the concept of Physical Law - the idea that there are representations possible which establish the boundaries of Physical function. Is Physical Law malleable or is there just one objective Physical reality? Do the Buddhic Plane Entities adjust Physical Law?

The Buddhic Plane Entities can adjust Physical function unless it is against the Will of The Tao. In answer to this question, Physical laws which govern Physical Plane are somewhat malleable but not all the time. It is a concept which is just stretchy for humans. Physical

---

[15]Spinor - a geometrical mathematical object which is fundamental to quantum electrodynamics and quantum chromodynamics particle field theories. All spin one half particle wave functions are represented with spinor functions. This refers to a discussion of balancing field equations representing particles by adjusting a scalar field by whatever amount is required to obtain equality.

Plane Laws according to Taoic Will are perpetual - upheld by the Buddhic Plane Entities. We do not intentionally throw this curve at you to confuse you, but remember, the Will of The Tao is change. To the extent that we comprehend the power and function of Buddhic Entities we only know that they are in accord with the Will of The Tao at and in all time frames.

Tao Song.

HELLO EARTH, HOW ARE YOU

We all are aware that our technology is putting great stress on the environment.   The Earth's ecological systems are being affected. How is the Earth?   What are the major problems?
First, we wish to offer you this: The intent of all Soul Patterns is to alleviate the necessity for beginning the protracted process of developing a technologically advanced civilization again from the start. On this Mother planet the expansion of consciousness and the development of higher technology are directly related to one another. One of the higher goals for this planet and shis inhabitants is to achieve Balance between these two factors - **technology and spirituality.** If Balance occurs, all technology will automatically assure that no danger comes to the planet or any of shis living systems. Nor will technology which puts stress upon the Mother planet be conceived, pursued, or allowed. The Mother planet cooperates with this goal to the limits of Physical Plane Law.   However, the higher goal does not include sacrificing the Mother's life. The consciousness of the Mother planet shiself understands this.
The planet will not allow shiself to be made dead. Therefore, if the abuses and imbalances reach a critical mass point and endanger the Mother planet's life, the Mother planet acts to assure shis own survival. Shis switches the polar axis which neutralizes the Negativity. The humans are of course nearly eliminated if there is a polar shift.
Also occurring at this Now is the potential for what we call the Jump[16]. The technological advancement has reached the point where there can be an energy or vibrational shift, an up-gearing - the Transcendence to Mind Mechanics. This transcendence or Jump will Balance the ecological system which exists on the Mother.
This planet is essential to the continuance of a triad of ensouled species in this section of the galaxy. This triad's desire, and also that of the larger realm, is to prevent the technology which humans have developed from over running its ensouled species spiritual development. It is necessary to the function of The ALL THAT IS that the natural

---

[16]Jump - See chapter "Jump to Mind Mechanics".   A "dimension" increase in which all ensouled species have linear access to all former life experiences and new physical abilities which allow new technology to occur.

Balance of this planet occurs. The Jump to Mind Mechanics and the harmonious Balance with other living beings on all Mother planets will successfully avert a polar shift.

Technology and spiritual development are related?

As we stated, spirituality and technology depend on each other to attain the Jump to a higher Rate or vibration. You might call this a dimension change. It is complex to explain. We do not even know whether it can be explained with words. The inter-relationship between the two factors is what occurs on this Mother planet. The advancement of technology must mirror the advancement of spirituality. All ensouled species on this Mother, when Balanced, advance spiritually in proportion to the technological development. The Jump to Mind Mechanics can be attained when the technology is used to enhance and maintain the inherent ecological Balance of the entire planet and shis living systems.

Larger numbers of humans are becoming rapidly aware of the complexities and ramifications of technology which is out of "sync" with the Spiritual Consideration required for Balance of the planet. No longer is it valid or workable to seek knowledge simply for knowledge's sake, for that search creates only sterility. Knowledge can only be considered such when applied for the Harmony and Balance of all things that are of or on the Mother planet shiself. Then knowledge can serve as a catapult for the Jump to Mind Mechanics and Ecological Balance.

Again we say, the prevention of an axis tilt is what is desired. If there is a continuance of the "fouling of ones own nest", so to speak, the Mother will simply shift shis polar axis in order to neutralize all Negativity and all humans and their technology will begin again.

What you are saying then is that if we continue on the course of using hydrocarbons and cutting the forests, the ecology will soon be on the verge of collapse, and there will be a shift to restore Balance.

Exactly. The Mother will not allow shiself to be killed for shis is essential to the Universe.

We need to make some changes.

Correct. We would offer you this simple, but astounding concept. It is not a new concept, but we wish to present a new way to contemplate, and approach this necessity -a more circular, more long reaching way of thinking about the concept, **"Recycle"**.

Do you know that by observing the entirety of the Universe you can understand how to resolve every bit of errant technology which has damaged your Mother? It is true. What does the Universe do - with its raw material - within all its Systems? It Recycles! And out of that process of Recycling engenders more resources than it started with. Now we are not going to get into a discussion of the Second Law of Thermodynamics, as you know it, here, but this is in fact, true. The Universe wastes nothing. Your Mother planet wastes nothing. The Mother's Living Systems, when in Balance, waste nothing. All is Recycled! Think on the intricacy and magnitude of this. Then you will know how to start as an individual. You will know what to do and what not to do as an individual. Analyze a living system and you will understand the Law of Recycle.... **"Only use that which can be returned as a resource within your own lifetime."**

Is the recycling of Physical things, matter, similar to the recycling of Souls?

All in the Whole of Whole, in The Tao, in The ALL THAT IS, whether in Physical Plane or in Non-Physical Plane function is continually recycled. There is never degeneration, or loss. In other words the concept of Entropy[17] is not functional in the Greater Reality. This may appear to be a contradiction according to "science" and what can be casually observed in Nature, but never the less it is true. The Universe and Tao is, "IS", perpetual abundance, life and expansion. In the Greater Reality the whole is greater than the sum of its parts. The parts augment the whole and continued recycling augments each part without taxing any of the natural resources. That concept: "sum", augments all the parts and the Whole - Physical and Spiritual. Do you see?

Yes, for example, life is a cycle, not a linear progression. As a whole, human beings control the destiny of the planet with the thoughts that they hold in their minds and the realities that those

---

[17]Entropy - In thermodynamics entropy is a measure of the ability of a system to do work. In natural processes there is a statistical extension of the concept - "There is a tendency for processes to proceed towards a state of disorder." In such processes there is always a loss; a loss of ability to do work, a loss of structure, a loss of identifiable differences. Evolution, for example, is an apparent contradiction to entropy since more complex structures are created by the system. However, if the system includes the energy input from sunlight then there is no contradiction.

become. Is that correct?

Correct. One of The Taoic Laws for Physical Plane is: **That into which you place your thought energy becomes your reality.**

Is there another intelligent species existing along side of us on this planet? Perhaps an ocean species?

There are two indigenous ensouled species on this Mother. The Homo Sapien Sapien are ensouled, able to contemplate linear thought processes - aware. The Cetacean group is also ensouled, conscious of self, aware of their own existence within the conscripts of linear time. There are some other species which are nearly evolved to the level of ensoulment but not completely so at this Now. Only Homo Sapiens and Cetaceans (whales, dolphins, and porpoises) at this Now.

The sapient creatures on any Mother create the outcomes and potentials of that living Mother planet. But, only to the point where the creators put their Mother's life in jeopardy. If the Mother's very life is in jeopardy, shis consciousness will prevent shis own death. But, to return to the original question, Yes, you are one of the two indigenous creator species for this Mother planet.

It sounds like the situation is precarious. It could go either way?

Yes.

Let's review the Physical and Spiritual aspects of the earth which provide a context from which to understand the situation.

As we have stated, the trauma the Mother planet suffers at this Now, is great. Collective human effort to effect Balanced, Considerate[18] thought and technology is required immediately.

Unless Considerate and deliberate attention is undertaken immediately, unless there is a collective human effort to re-enter the Balanced system, to work as an integral part of the system of the planet's function, within twenty five to fifty of your years, the damage to the planet will be so great that the Mother will simply shrug, shift shis axis, and Balance these injuries and inconsiderations.

In other words, the planet will make a polar shift. The resultant energies thus released you might well call - Holocaust. This action would neutralize all Negative energies and actions and Balance the

---

[18]Considerate - See chapter "Energizing Positive Action".

planet. Two percent of the humans will possibly survive. Nearly all technology would, again, return to the primitive.

However, it is important to understand that this potential scenario is as easily and as surely resolved as it is continued toward further imbalance. Human's thoughts and actions do have a direct affect upon the Mother's physical health. Therefore a collective decision to change the thoughts people energize, and how these thoughts are put into action, can precipitate a successful resolve.

We have previously discussed what we call the principle of Beneficial Wholism Assessment[19]. It is known by all that if you sever a section from a circle you no longer have a circle. It is the same with any system, whether it is a system of thought, a system of action, or a living ecological system. If Beneficial Wholism Assessment is not a goal of each functioning part of a system, that system will collapse. Also, the collapse will certainly be very uncomfortable to experience while it is happening.

Beneficial Wholism Assessment is contemplating and analyzing whether or not an action or a thought will have on-going validity for all linear time frames, and all beings functioning within linear time frames.

For example, if a tree is cut, it is important to understand that before that decision is made, Beneficial Wholism Assessment must be applied. Ask: If this tree is cut, will it be a good thing for the tree, will it be a good thing for me? Will it be a good thing for the living things residing in the area of this tree? Can it be replaced doubly? Can its role within the environmental system be reinstated "Within the Length of One Human Lifetime?"

Not only do those questions need to be considered at the moment, but the ramifications of the possible action must be considered. What will be the affects to me, to people, to the area, and other living things one hundred years from now if this tree is cut? If a decision is assessed and deemed to be Beneficial now, and in one hundred years from now, it is a decision which is potentially within the Balance and the Consideration of the system, it is a workable decision to put to action.

The main factor to remember, for those who want to apply Beneficial Wholism Assessment, is that it is not possible, in many situations, to halt that which has already occurred. If a tree has been

---

[19]See chapter "Energizing Positive Action".

cut, anguish will not uncut that tree.

However, it is eminently possible to initiate new modes of thinking, of action, and of Balanced technology so that forward action will produce Balanced ways of replenishment, cleanup, and healing. We are meaning this: It is not possible to un-discover fission reactors. It is not possible to unmake foams or plastics. However, it is possible to develop Balanced thinking, actions, and technology which can resolve the anomalies that those technologies have produced.

Once again remember, within a Balanced system there is no waste. All things made within Nature's system are returned, reprocessed and expanded to the benefit of the whole system. So, in one aspect, or from one point of view, the Universe and the Mother planet is one huge recycling machine.

It is beneficial to create technologies that produce only that which can be recycled into continued resources. The recycling process produces continual expansion; like a balloon which is continually expanding. Recycled energy, in conjunction with thought and action, created by humans in Balance with their system, creates continuous new energy for the expansion and continuation of the Universe, which includes the Greater Reality of The Tao Itself.

Does the Earth have a spirit that can detect the humans and their intentions? Can the Mother planet determine whether or not things are becoming out of Balance?

The Mother has a level of consciousness. It is tied in with other stellar bodies; you might say, with solar systems, galaxies, and Universes. So, if you say a galaxy or a Universe has a Soul, an awareness of universal connectedness, with reserve, we would say, Yes. However, individual Soul Patterns create thought energy. You are the creators of material reality.

The Mother planet has awareness of shis own essentiality within the scheme of things. Within that consciousness is the knowledge of the Physical Law: **The least easily replenished pieces within the system must be the most guarded.** Therefore, since human Souls are not in jeopardy of extinction, the choice is to save shiself when humans create critical imbalance. This choice ensures that there will be more opportunities for Soul Patterns to reenter; there will be a habitable planet available.

Souls are recycled. In other words they come back.

Correct. Soul Patterns return to the Physical Plane until all that is available to learn and experience has been accomplished.

As long as there is a planet to come back to?
Exactly.

Otherwise, the majority of humans go with the planet.
Correct again. The necessity of Balance within the larger system is to be greatly considered, because all habitable systems depend upon each other for Balance.

In other words, there is a Balance between the various solar systems on a much larger scale than we can perceive.
Correct. That is why this Mother is to receive intense efforts of assistance.

In mechanics theory, one sometimes assigns a wavelength proportional to the size of the object. I'm a certain height so I have a certain wavelength. By assigning a speed to the wave a frequency is then defined. The earth is considerably larger than I am so its wavelength could be longer and frequency lower. That could mean that its consciousness operates at a slower Rate in terms of our Rate as human beings. Is this correct?
Yes, you are correct. The Planet's rate is not only slower, it is fatter. In comparison to the function of the human body, the inhale and exhale - The Mothers inhale may last ten thousand years. Do you see?

In other words its whole life cycle is at a different, much "slower" Rate than ours, as humans?
Correct.

Do other planets in the solar system have consciousness? Lets say Mars for example. Does Mars have a consciousness like that of Earth?
Mars has it's own Planet consciousness. Yes.

Is The Tao monitoring the planet's condition?
Of course. The Tao is also the planet as the planet is part of the functioning body of The Tao.

Is man basicly responsible for the extinction of most of the extinct species over the last several hundred thousand years?

Sometimes, there have simply been cancellations. Humans have made many species extinct. But, there have been some which simply were not practical or workable within the system of this planet. This may seem far-fetched, you might say, but some species have been phased out. The Buddhic Plane Entities have dominion over hive species and can institute development of new species or phase out ones that are not workable, or practically adaptable for reasons of behavior, sustenance, or space. Many threatened wildlife species are now being observed and assessed by humans at the turning point towards recovery as opposed to extinction. The most important factor is that a much greater degree of cooperation and international projects are occurring. There is unity occurring.

Who makes the decision whether or not a species should be phased out? Does The Tao make these decisions?

It is a cooperative decision between The Tao and the Buddhic Planes Entities. Referring to the previous discussion, it is a Beneficial Wholism Assessment, which considers the specific planet itself. But it is the Buddhic Entities who make the decision; of course, in complete accord with Taoic Will.

You mentioned a blueprint plan in connection with spiritual aspects of the Mother. Could you elaborate on that plan?

The blueprint is The Taoic Law for this planet - what The Tao needs for this planet and shis human species.

And what is the Law?

That Physical Plane technology on this planet will be correlated, be reflective of, and Balanced with Spiritual advancement. That these factors be completed to the joyful advantage of all other systems on this planet, it's solar system, galaxy, and Universe.

Does The Taoic Law, in respect to the Mother Earth, apply to other planets that have life on them?

Each living Mother planet has its own variant of this Taoic Law, Yes.

According to our laws of physics every action has a reaction, so consideration and inconsideration are tied to one another. If we develop our technology and our spirituality lags, then we suffer the

automatic consequences of that.

Correct, The First Law of The Tao is: **All is One.**
Therefore, Balance is required.

And Balance might not be immediate. It might be long term, in terms of our linear time, but it will come. Correct?

That is quite correct. That is what is happening at this Now. You are experiencing the results of a world in which technology has developed more rapidly than spirituality. Machines have been held in higher regard than Beneficial Wholism Assessment. At this Now, there is a great striving to bridge that gap. Within The Whole of the Whole, regarding Physical Plane function, the intent - the desire to Balance - is being energized with great intensity. In other words, because humans are showing a great desire to Balance spirituality with technology for their Mother planet, they are being given as great an opportunity as possible to succeed. Many levels of beings are participating in this effort.

Why don't we learn from of our mistakes? If many Soul Patterns have been around previously, why hasn't the current population learned? Are there just too few Soul Patterns trying to help? Could you elaborate on that? If highly advanced past civilizations ended in polar shifts because they were out of sync with Mother Nature, why haven't we learned our lesson?

We do not mean to seem glib or judgmental, but how do know that you have not learned?

I see your point. We may have already learned and not realize it just yet.

We wish to state: The chance for this specific civilization to Balance and therefore accomplish the Rate Jump is much greater than any other civilization which has reached the same crisis point. Do you see?

I think so. You are saying we have a good chance.

Correct. And if that occurs then The Jump will be accomplished and the planet's inhabitants will increase a Rate or Dimension.

Does this mean we will become enlightened as a species?

And change Rates, yes.

A faster frequency?
    Correct. A faster Rate is a more expanded perspective.

So, we now have an opportunity to make the Jump to the next plane of consciousness. If we can Balance our spiritual energies with our advanced technology and be in Harmony with the planet, we will expand and transcend and we will never have to deal with this problem again?
    Correct, for the planet will also transcend to the next Rate. Within that increased Rate only Balanced function is possible.

So we need to change the thought patterns of governments. Instead of putting people on Mars they need to refocus energies and desires on what we try to do here, to go back to helping the Mother Earth and slow down our technology.
    Please understand this important factor. Re-think the statement you just made. If developments in technology are slowed, there will not be enough time to heal that which is needing to be healed. Therefore, the technology must go forth at an <u>increased</u> rate. But the decision to use Beneficial Wholism Assessment while developing and instituting that technology, will more quickly close the gap between technology and spirituality and make healing possible.

Then in a practical sense we are in a technological race as well as a spiritual race. We need to develop the type of technology that can sustain an on going process, support all the people, and at the same time reduce the environmental damage.
    Correct, and rectify the damage done prior to the realization that the Recycle Law is essential. The most beneficial concept to energize is not weaponry but livingry, The Fuller has said that, R. Buckminster Fuller[20]. Then you can see that space investigation is definitely an aspect of livingry. It is the manufacture of weaponry and socio-economic systems based on the manufacture of weaponry which is contrary to Beneficial Wholism Assessment.

Who is The Fuller?

---

[20]R. Buchminster Fuller, <u>Critical Path</u>, c 1981 Fuller St. Martin's Press, 1981.

Richard Buckminster Fuller is a Speaker [21], also a great mathematician, inventor, philosopher, and developer of the tetrahedron dome, geodesic dome. Shis also, developed the first totally self sustaining and self-contained design for a single family dwelling and then a city. Shis is, in your terms, a genius of potentials.

So, the obvious but very difficult task is to channel the resources into advancing our standard of living instead of channelling them into weapon systems.
Correct, and that, as you have stated, requires unification of thought, intent, and action.

Well, we are seeing very promising trends in the political systems right now. As a whole however, we need to change many people's thought processes - their awareness of the situation - so they can promote healing of the earth.
Correct.

Is it possible to make a mental broadcast to everybody in the world? For example, I might send the thought "recycle" to everyone in the world. Is that within the possibilities allowed by The Taoic Law or do each one of us have to work on it individually?
It is possible to do both. The answer to your question, both questions, is Yes. Each person must evolve as an individual. However, an agreement between individuals to energize that which is agreed upon has incredible energy potential to effect and move other people who need to change. Therefore, if the message you wish to send is "recycle", group meditation with those who wish to transmit that concept twice a week for even five minutes can have incredible impact. The group meditation can create energy which carries, transmits, and enhances that message.

Can this be amplified?
The energy created during a group meditation can be augmented by a clear crystal. Each can use shis own, or one crystal can be used in the center of a circle around which the meditators are seated.

---

[21] Speaker - A person who is a "herald" of the times. A person who comes to spark great advances and changes.

A quartz crystal?

Yes, or a diamond or a Herkimer[22] diamond. Clear is more beneficial. Colored crystals are more complex and require more expertise. Whether or not you choose to use a crystal to augment thought, energize and speak to others of energizing what they want to have, not what they do not want. The ideal is a Balanced environment and a healthy planet. Think as if it were already accomplished. Visualize the Mother in shis ideal state. That kind of mind energy creates the potential for the healthy vision to become reality.

Tao Song.

---

[22]Herkimer Diamonds are specific to New York State. They have a much greater hardness than common quartz crystals and many are exceptionally clear.

THE FORESTS AND AGRICULTURE

We would like to talk with you about the environment, and the environmental damage to the planet. What is the most significant factor that is offending the planet?

There is not enough priority nor understanding regarding trees.

The cutting of mature long standing trees is the single most offensive and damaging factor which is occurring. By destroying the forests you are destroying yourselves.

We do not mean to sound so conclusive. We mean you are hastening the potential for your own demise. The trees are the air makers and they are also the air purifiers. They are the filters for the atmosphere envelope of this Mother.

Therefore, when one mature tree is cut, two yearling trees are needed to replace it. Of course it is beneficial to replace a greater number than two for one, but two for one is crucial. That is the fewest replacement number required to ensure the safety of the atmosphere envelope.

Two extra trees in everyone's backyard would be a great benefit. Many more trees in residential areas would be of great assistance. Trees in areas where people live make the air within that area more healthy. Trees can spot purify the air of small areas.

There has been a considerable increase in the last ten or fifteen years in deforestation. You no doubt have noticed this. Do we need to do something on that end?

It is very difficult to grapple with things which have already occurred. It is difficult to confront "hen scratchings" on paper; "fight city hall" and wade through "red tape".

The most beneficial thing is to organize and encourage tree planting groups, or even plant a tree yourselves. If every person found one spot to plant one tree once a week, within six months you could recoup the damage. You could begin to heal the oxygen envelope. Not of course completely clean, but turned around so that active filtration is going toward the Positive.

There is currently a controversy in the lumber industry over tree farming. Tree farming is essentially the idea of taking a spot of land and growing trees like you grow corn. Usually a monoculture with

pesticides, and so on. How does tree farming fit in?

The factor to consider is this - establishing priorities. Can products that trees provide be as easily provided from other sources than trees? Re-orienting priorities and how people interact to the function of trees is more important. Which? That is the question to ask. Which is more important, paper towels or trees?

The tree farming can be functional in ensuring that the future will have paper towels and wood for structures. However, the stands of mature trees are the essential factor for the health of this Mother. There are alternate construction materials. There are many things which are as great in beauty as cut wood, but there are few things as beautiful and as essential as a living, breathing forest. It is all priorities.

When you mean everyone, lets see, there are five to six billion people on the planet. So we need to plant fifty to one hundred billion trees to start to turn it around.

Correct. Even in this country, if everyone planted one tree per week the air quality of this - planet quadrant, could be improved immensely.

Last year a group to which we belong planted several thousand trees in the watershed of the city reservoir. An obstacle to continuing the planting of trees in the watershed is that the city council will not give up the option of logging in the watershed.

Do you feel that it is still viable to plant the watershed?

Yes.   However, some people are reluctant to plant trees in the watershed under those conditions.

The main factor, the primary priority, is being overlooked. No matter how long the trees are in the ground, it is better than not planting. If planting trees is contingent upon ceasing the logging, soon there will be a bare watershed.

Do trees have any other function besides air filtration?

Trees are the purifiers, the circulating units; They are also the link between air and water. Therefore loss of trees render not only poor air quality, but less water also.   It is important to re-familiarize yourselves with the transpiration process of trees; to understand the water and gas exchange process within the Air/Tree/Water/Air cycle.

In a lumber production environment, there are different approaches

to harvesting the trees. One of them is to clear cut, which means cutting everything and taking it out. That is sometimes associated with tree farming. The idea is that they will replant and turn it into a farm if it is not one already. Another approach is to try to harvest the mature trees and essentially leave the forest ecology intact.

The latter is much more Wholistic providing that the second growth can achieve first growth size within one human lifetime and that careful attention is given to the required two for one when reforesting.

Can we expect an ecologically Balanced system to produce adequate lumber and fiber if we use a system which takes out the mature trees and lets the forest run in a natural way?

It is difficult for us to encourage or facilitate concepts or methods which assist humans to be detrimental to themselves or the Mother. There are enough wood products already available for building. It is not necessary to cut mature trees within the next five years in this entire country.

Do you mean stockpiled?

Yes, plus all wood products which can be recycled, and are not being recycled.

The most important concept in any Balanced system is that everything be **recycled**. No raw materials need be sacrificed within the system, until all that is recyclable has been recycled, or has changed form so completely that it is only usable in its new form.

Just last week I saw a building being burned down to dispose of it. The fire department used it for practice. It was a wood frame construction building and now that material is lost.

There you have an example about which we are speaking. It is no wonder that we have seen so many of you "Searchers" saddened to the point of tears over the methodic way people are injuring themselves.

Yes. This opportunity for recycling is a wonderful idea....

Not practical you are thinking?

Possibly. In order to give that aspect of recycling impetus it has to fit into our economic system. It has to be profitable. I could see how people might dismantle buildings and sell the materials at a profit. If someone started companies to do that, it might work out.

There. You have a solution. There is always a way to make

Balance profitable because in the end Balance profits all. It is over use of raw materials, through fear of scarcity, which causes the system to become out of Balance.

We are still considering the tree farming aspect and the ramifications on the industry, the economy. If tree farms are deemed essential because pulp products are desired, tree farms are workable provided Beneficial Wholism Assessment[23] is applied to tree farm management. However, we think it is perplexing to clear cut an area which has trees in order to plant trees. It is contradictory and self destructive. Therefore, tree farms which do not require standing trees be cut would be a Positive.

Though it is quite difficult to stop people from cutting trees that provide them with their income, it is easy to tell people that they do not need to stop. They only need take a small percentage of their time and put back something. In other words plant trees to replace those which are cut.

It is important to encourage this line of thought. It is much easier to encourage people to take Positive action than attempt to stop or prevent a thing which is already in motion. Apply focus to the healing process itself: planting, cleanup, recycling; whatever Positive actions are used in the healing of the planet. That focus will show the greater masses where their errors lie. The old methods which cause harm or pollution will atrophy quickly. People who are energetically attempting to bind the wounds set a Positive example, an example which encourages those who are causing injury to re-think their actions.

Let's talk about reducing the demand for lumber and pulp products. Recycling would obviously help out with the lumber.

Correct. One of the most effective building materials is available to all, with care, of course. It is earth. Bricks, but more lightly baked brick, not so highly baked that it becomes brittle. There is nothing that can insulate as well as earth mixed with grasses and then baked or pounded. This medium is also flexible in terms of tension.

There are considerations, of course. You would not want to build large skyscrapers with bricks. However, to panel the entire inside of a home with wood is unnecessary. For some of the structure, yes, but the greatest amount of the waste is in decor, as you say. Other materials

---

[23]See the chapter "Energizing Positive Action" for a discussion of Beneficial Wholism Assessment.

can be as decorative and much less damaging. This concept is what we are offering for consideration.

I see. In other words instead of using wood siding, use brick siding.
Yes, or sculpted earth; rammed earth.

Are there any other areas to discuss regarding forestry?
We would offer this. It is important to begin with the smalls, the children. One of the most effective methods to effect change is to initiate the concept, or ritual, of "**taboo**". Each small is encouraged to understand that it is nearly an unspeakable crime to cut a tree.

Attitudes regarding trees and all natural resources could be greatly changed using this "**taboo**" concept. Then you would find that choice of what resources to use would be assessed with greater amount of Consideration.   When Consideration becomes an integral part of people's thought processes, then large changes can be effected.

Let's talk about planting trees. That is something we can do that is very Positive. What kind of trees should we be planting?   The original forests have a complex variety of trees and they grow in different stages. Some become dominant in early stages and others are dominant later in the evolution of a forest.
Choose among those species which are native to that area. But, at this Now choose the most rapid growth trees. Use trees which put out a greater degree of foliage. Try for trees with less height and more circumference. For the Northern area of this continent, evergreen trees are the ones which are most Beneficial for the Mother. They are the ones which are being rapidly depleted.

Which species are preferable?
Cedars are smilely. The broad flat needle is very efficient. Yes. There are many species of pine and spruce. Low growing evergreens can also be of great benefit; Pfitzer and Sergeant junipers. With a large smile, we will say this - we do not mean to seem intensely biased, but from the way we see trees, you can never go wrong with a Redwood. They have such shardy[24] patterns.

So in an area where Redwood trees have grown before it might be

---

[24] Shardy - beautiful - full of light - shards of light.

a good idea to plant Redwoods.
      Correct.

Would it be a good idea to mix them up, Redwoods and Cedars together?
      It is very beneficial to study the entire complex of growth adjacent the area you wish to plant if you want to reestablish a larger area. However we see that at this Now simply encouraging people to plant the kind of tree they love best will at least get them motivated. Evergreens for this quadrant are the most efficient.

Is it imperative to take immediate action or can we let industry and agriculture continue as is until a cumulative commitment for sound ecological practice develops.
      We wish to state that immediate action, even if you could return to yesterday and act then, would not be to soon.

Currently and previously, a vast amount of forest land has been converted to agricultural lands. Are there areas in the world where it would be wise to reverse this process?
      The large stands of evergreens in the Northern Hemisphere should be preserved intact if at all possible. The jungle stands in the Southern Hemisphere should be given immediate attention and assistance to reforest. Especially in the Amazon basin. The large remaining stands in the continent of Africa and in Asia should be kept intact.

People could buy the land and put it aside as preserve.
      That is a very practical possibility.

Also people could buy land, reforest it, and then sell it but with restrictions with respect to the trees and forest.
      That is also feasible. It is a pragmatic way to function within the legal system which exists in this Now.

The forest practices in the United States are largely determined by economics. For example, the tree farming returns eight percent, which is an acceptable return (for most companies). Many people argue that the tree farming approach merely passes on the full cost to future generations. Again, an economic argument. In any event economics are very important to all. What can we do to align the economic incentives with ecologically sound forestry?

Get your priorities straight. It is not that there is not enough.
It is a matter of distribution. It is procrastination and indecision which
eats up the money and resources.

**How could we get the lumber companies to not cut trees? How can
we make it economically feasible not to cut? For example instead of
clear cutting because they have to maximize revenues maybe they
could be rewarded in some other way. I was thinking in terms of
some business incentive. The only revenue they really get is net
profit from the tree after all the costs. If they get paid not to cut the
tree then there is no operating cost. Is there something in this area?**
Go directly to the source. However, it is not possible to
organize enough monetary enticement not to cut trees if there is still
large demand for lumber in building. Therefore, it is possibly more
effective to entice the consumer not to use board lumber for anything
but structural essentials. In other words most lumber, especially
Redwood evergreens are cut for decorative purposes. If there are no
buyers there is no reason to cut the trees. The cutting of Redwoods
would halt all along the line.

**It has occurred to me that we could make a quantum jump in
technology and reduce the demand for forest products considerably.**
We send you a large smile. We do not ever wish to seem that
we are adverse to technology. In fact the most likely method people can
use to re-establish Balance for the Mother will be through increasing the
development of technology which is developed and employed using
Beneficial Wholism. You speak rightly when you say advance the
technology to effect these changes.

**So if we can improve technology to provide alternate materials for
lumber, be less destructive in the forest by developing Positive
technology, our situation would change.**
You are quite correct. The options and potentials become vast.
We wish to offer this observation. Sometimes people are so busy
looking for resources to "take", that they do not see what the Mother's
systems "give" them. We have watched and assessed the potential of
tree products and by-products which can be developed and recycled from
trees allowed to remain alive. Consider the natural waste products
which trees produce while still living - Outer bark which is shed, leaves,
and needles. There is enough material from these by-products to make
sufficient paper and presswood to alleviate the need to cut trees by

nearly two thirds. This is an idea which could be outlined and presented to the wood and paper industries.

In other words, instead of cutting the trees down they would actually....
Harvest the by-products trees produce naturally.

Harvest natural wood products which fall on the forest floor?
Correct.   Also there are many species of heavy outer bark producing trees which shed large quantities of bark. This can be taken or trimmed; the outer bark. If it is done with care it will not harm the living trees.   By doing this, it is possible to train some species of evergreens to accelerate their outer bark production.

Is there anything else that you have looked into and observed with regard to trees that you would like to share with us?
There is a group of individuals increasing in number whose intent is to purchase square miles of land so that the forest and terrain is under private control.   This may not seem to be a feasible or a practical avenue for results.   However, think of purchasing six square feet of land, or "one tree" parcel. This is being taken into consideration. In actuality it is quite feasible.   The more land or tree parcels owned by private individuals who love trees, the fewer trees are available to cut.

We wish you to consider this also.   If all nations refuse to purchase wood products, then trees will no longer be a possibility for income. People, out of necessity, will become open to alternate income possibilities.   If there is no profit in cutting trees, it would be stopped.

We wish to point out also, that tree density in one area can have a direct effect upon air quality so far away it may seem totally unrelated. We wish to use the Amazon basin and the Amazon rain forests as an example.   This area is critical to the entire planet, as you know. However there is a direct correlation between the Amazon basin and the air quality in Japan.   You can verify this directly by watching the Earth's ocean temperatures and the air currents between those two locations and how they have changed as trees were eliminated.   The more trees that are eliminated in the Amazon basin the greater the pollution becomes in the Islands of Japan.
This information, although potentially alarming, is not given to depress or discourage you. Dear ones, do not become frustrated with the

intricate disparities. Do not become overwhelmed by the complexity of the situation. Remember the people of one small organization in terms of percentages of the total planet population succeeded in stopping the murder of the Great Whales. It is also possible to save the trees and yourselves.

Simply do not cut wood. Although you can not prevent another's actions, short of using force, alter your own behavior. You can choose action which neutralizes those which are Negative or detrimental.

What is happening to the soil in which our food is grown? Is there a problem with our soil?
Salts.

Can you explain that a little? Irrigation perhaps.
Correct. Irrigation and artificial fertilizers. There are also soil problems because farmers are growing crops which are not indigenous to the specific growing area.

Are there any other excessive minerals besides salts.
We wish to state that there is an alkaloid[25] build-up in the soil throughout many areas. This is a result of soil reaction to additives used to enhance or suppress various plant growth;   artificial fertilizers, herbicides, and pesticides.

These were brought in to increase crop productivity.
Correct. The intent behind the development of these chemicals was Positive, but Beneficial Wholism Assessment of potential effects was over-looked.

In the long run do these increase productivity or decrease productivity because the land is depleted?
It is not so much becoming depleted. It is becoming saturated. There are so many additives in the soil for farming that the bacteria which maintain healthy soil cannot process the overload. The soils are so over conditioned that farming areas can not nurture crops without continued manipulation. The important factor to understand is that the introduction of plants which cannot acclimate is the first step toward soil

---

[25]An alkaloid is an organic salt.

imbalance. Then artificial means are required in order to sustain those plants. Therefore the method most Beneficial for the soil is to plant crops indigenous to the specific area.

Is there a way of making farming more practical for the general population and still observe the natural soil Balance?
      Yes.   Assess carefully and with Consideration, enhancing substances.   Use those which are less cumulatively residual. Also contemplate the potential of hydroponics.

What are some methods to correct the soil other than the ones you mentioned?
      Introduce indigenous plant life and allow natural climatic conditions. Say a semi-arid to desert - although it may be rich farm land when water is added, naturally there is not that much water. Therefore, to correct the metabolism and chemistry of a certain soil area reintroduce indigenous plants: scrub, creosote or beechwood, cactus, sage, etc., and allow these to grow sustained by natural precipitation. Within a period of five to seven years the reconditioned area could then again be farmed with "Considerate" or augmented methods.

It could be farmed using indigenous crops?
      It could be farmed again with irrigation and foreign plants. However, every five to seven years introduce only indigenous plants for an equal amount of time to maintain Balance.

Is it possible for a person to fulfill their diet requirements from plants from within the area where they live?
      This is where distribution is a factor which plays an important role. For some areas, the answer is yes to your question. In other areas it is not possible.   These factors lead to the quantity of human population.

Could you clarify this?
      In some areas there are too many people for the farm territory to sustain sufficient crops with what can be grown in a specific territory. This culture is no longer a hunter-gatherer culture that can survive on what is available within twenty to one hundred and fifty square miles. The land no longer supplies adequate indigenous and yet Balanced diet for the amount of population at this Now. Again we offer the potential of hydroponic technology. This could be of great benefit, produce

sufficient food, still be in Harmony with the soil, and satisfy traditional forms of agriculture.

Tao Song.

THE ATMOSPHERE

We would like to focus on the atmosphere. One thing very prominent in the news is the depletion of the ozone layer. If that layer depletes to a certain degree, the increased ultraviolet radiation will cause harm to plant life. If this occurs, trees will be harder to grow. There is, apparently, a large hole in the ozone layer over the Antarctic continent. Has this ozone hole always existed? Is it man made? How can we stop it? How can we reduce ozone depletion? Is it really something that we should pay attention to, or are our scientists over reacting?

The actual situation is a combination of many of these factors which you have stated. Some scientists are definitely over reacting. There is a relationship between fluorocarbons and the ozone layer. It is not as great as is thought, however. Over the eons there have been fluctuations in the ozone layer over the polar caps because the severe temperatures. The composition and the quantity of ice tends to draw ozone out of the atmosphere like a sponge. This is why the ozone density is much less at the poles. In connection with what we have discussed together previously, if a large quantity of polar ice was melted and the fresh water dispersed into the oceans a release of captured ozone, frozen ozone, would occur. In connection with this, the additional fresh water and resulting clouds would encourage incredible storm activity. This increased storm activity brings with it the producer of ozone - **lightening**. Therefore, the ozone content of the atmosphere is still retrievable. The atmosphere is not past the point of reclamation.

Is the production and release of the fluorocarbon compounds by man a significant factor?

It does have a detrimental effect. But, there has been a great consciousness conversion. The slightly exaggerated panic over the ozone layer contributed to this consciousness raising. People now know not to use aerosol fluorocarbon products. Therefore the depletion of atmospheric ozone is not reaching a critical stage as rapidly as many have predicted.

Based on what you say, I would conclude that we should proceed with the elimination of fluorocarbons.

It is definitely good to do so. You are correct.

We have a little longer than we thought, but we still have to eliminate the fluorocarbon products?

Correct. Think how many mechanical devices operate with the compound freon[26]. This compound is one of the greatest causes of the degeneration of ozone.

How much has the atmosphere changed over the last fifty million years. There must have been considerable plant life fifty million years ago and the oxygen level has changed to some degree. The oxygen level is about 20 percent now. Is there any thing to discuss regarding this?

There are natural and man made conditions which cause increases and decreases in the percentage of oxygen in the atmosphere. The optimum norm of the most Balanced eras, including previous technological civilizations, averages twenty seven to twenty nine percent. There have been times in previous civilizations when the oxygen percentage has been a low as ten point two. This is below critical function levels however, and did not remain at that level for more than five years. The Planet rebalances shiself so that all living forms are not lost. In these situations polar shifts re-establish Balance.

Based on the optimum percentage you gave us we are considerably below that?

The ozone is somewhat lower, but as we assess the on-going statistics, it is increasing somewhat. There has been a rapid decline in the oxygen level until approximately five years ago - closer to three years ago. The percentage of oxygen in the atmosphere has dropped three points in the last twenty five years.

It would seem that such a dramatic drop would be obvious to scientific measure. Yet over the last twenty five years the consensus is that the oxygen level has always been around twenty percent (standard value = 20.95 percent). Can you explain this?

There is no frame of reference or precedent for scientists working within this field. The few scientists studying the percentage differentiations of oxygen have not been given credence. It is not until now, when the air quality of the people functioning day to day became

---

[26]Freon - a halocarbon refrigerant used in the cooling systems of air conditioners, refrigerators, freezers, etc.

so obviously changed, that investigations have been instituted. Quality had to become so depleted that individual health was threatened before the scientific majority would give credence to those few who realized what was occurring.

When you speak of a three percent decline, do you mean the oxygen level decreased from twenty two plus percent to twenty percent?
Wait.... We are receiving corrected data within ourselves. There are fluctuations over the last twenty five years.

This is the corrected assessment. The average decrease has been point zero seven five percent (.075%) per year until three years ago.[27] At fifteen years previous there is no drop for that year. At twenty one years previous there is no drop for that year. All other years are dropping point zero seven five.

It is apparent that only in recent time has the percentage dropped significantly.
Correct.

We have attempted to check on the oxygen content of the atmosphere and we were not successful after a day of checking for published measurements. The few that were contacted stated categorically that the oxygen percentage is just 20.95 percent and that is that. No further measurements are required. What is the actual percentage of oxygen in the our backyard[28] today, to at least one decimal place. By oxygen we mean molecular oxygen, or the symbol O2. There are other oxygen atoms in the air such as water H2O and carbon dioxide CO2 and those types of gases. We would not count those.
You are thinking of viable breathable O2 not extraneous gases percentage.

Right. The percentage we want is the count of oxygen molecules in a given volume. Then give a count of all the other gas molecules and get the total. Divide the oxygen molecules by the total gas

---

[27]This numerical assessment was given in November of 1989.

[28]In Willits, California on December 7, 1990.

molecules and multiply by one hundred. This will give you the percentage.

At this Now, in your backyard the total percentage of one cubic meter of atmosphere contains an oxygen percentage of 19.99762

You must have counted all the molecules. That was to five decimal places.

You would find yesterday there was a fluctuation to 20.2013 percent.

We will need to correct these numbers for water vapor. What was the humidity.

Is it viable to count the water vapor? This is an essential part of the planets functioning available oxygen. This is also essential.

Yes, but the standard value is referenced to a dry air basis.

The day of the nineteen point nine percent oxygen reading there is 33.6 percent humidity. On the twenty point two day it is 28.5 percent.

We will also need the associated temperatures.

The temperature on the nineteen point nine day is a high of 72 degrees and on the twenty point two day is 66 degrees.

That is quite a variation in a single day, .2 percent[29].

It is. Taking into consideration the oxygen levels in your local vicinity, the pollutants, the other factors in air quality, it would be quite shocking to take a reading on a hot humid day in July in Southern California. The available oxygen levels are alarmingly low.

What is the current percent oxygen, breathable O2, of one cubic meter of air in our back yard today, January 8, 1992? Also, what is associated humidity and temperature needed to calculate the dry air percentage?

---

[29]Corrected for humidity, the percentages per mass of dry air are 20.19 and 20.13 percent or a difference of .14 percent.

It is 19.796[30] percent oxygen. The temperature is 39 degrees F with 31.5 percent humidity at 8:00 a.m. this day.

An important aspect of the atmospheric process that we have not talked about is the water vapor cycle and how that is affected.
What you call global weather patterns.

Yes, and how the weather patterns are affected by what we are doing.
As we have previously stated, all factors in a system affect all other factors in that system.

There has been a drought for several years in California. However, recently there has been more rain.
It is possible for many people to reshape weather patterns through their thoughts and choices. Everyone in California got tired of being dry, therefore, rain. So many people were energizing rain that it accumulated enough focused energy to bring that into reality. It is also important to remember that the weather patterns are affected by pollutants and non-recycling as much as any other part of the ecosystem. We do not feel that the weather is irreversibly in a trend towards the thinning of the atmosphere envelop of this Mother. However, it is a possibility.   One important factor, in terms of weather, is being overlooked. Weather trends and patterns change or redirect themselves over long long periods of linear time. One factor that many are not observing is the acclimation factor. People have introduced non-native plants into areas which can not sustain these plants without artificial or remade weather in the form of irrigation or cultured plants.   More attention must be paid to an area's natural weather patterns. Most of the south-eastern portion of California is naturally very arid to desert. The deliberate transformation of this natural pattern, which is coordinated within the whole of the area's system, has caused great imbalance. For though the weather patterns have stayed nearly the same, the slight changes are much more intense for the plants. People have a vested interest in keeping non-acclimated plants alive. The other great factor affecting weather patterns is population stress. This becomes acute when

---

[30]Corrected for humidity, the oxygen percentage per mass of dry air is 19.828 percent. This is over one percent below the accepted standard value of 20.95 percent.

a land area is asked to support more people than the natural environment can accomplish.

The southern costal areas of California have a very large population. Although there are known problems with the soil, the irrigated central valley area is very productive.

All these factors play an integral part on the fluctuations in global weather patterns.

What is the impact? How is the weather altered in that arid region of California?

The Mother's energies will attempt to normalize these stressed areas. One way of accomplishing this is a radical change in weather patterns.

Would that mean that because it was once an arid area that has since been irrigated there would be a trend towards drought?

Yes. It is a kind of hint given to people by the Mother and also a self preservation relief valve for the Mother.

It would seem that forest practices would also have a large impact on the weather.

There can be a large upset in the gas Balance of the air, the elements oxygen, nitrogen, etc. Then the potential becomes clear. The over population would be resolved quickly. Trees, the atmospheric filters, are being removed. The turbulence and changing air currents because of different combinations on different levels of the atmosphere could cause incredible weather changes - the heralding of the shift. That is why we have emphasized the importance of trees.

The CO_2 levels are rising in the atmosphere. That has been measured extensively. Is it combustion that is lowering the content of oxygen?

It is the destruction of efficient and inherent filtering systems. It is the destruction of the living organisms which produce oxygen. It is interesting to note that the volcanic eruptions which have been occurring are proving to be a great safety valve against the purported global warming trend. It is now assumed that the amount of ash in the atmosphere has successfully reduced overall temperatures 2.5 to 4.0 degrees F.

Trees produce oxygen.

Correct. Also the oceans' plant systems produce oxygen. Kelp is a major contributor of oxygen and processor of CO_2. The demise of the kelp forests contributes greatly to the decrease in oxygen percentages in the atmosphere. The Enedswr of the ocean, the whales and dolphins, have managed the ecological Balance of their habitat more efficiently than Terrans, land humans, have managed their territory. For though the oceans are reaching levels of distress, the damage there is not as great as the land area deterioration. It is the time for Terrans to become as wise in the ways of Balance as the Cetaceans.

How much oxygen, in percentage, does the ocean produce versus the trees? Is it, say, half of the available oxygen , or a third, or two thirds?

It is important to understand that each area is tied to the active function of the other area. The by-products produced by trees: pollens, scent molecules and other exhalents are essential to the oxygen producing plants of the ocean. There is also, you see - and this is verifiable scientifically - a kind of land plant - ocean plant inter communication. There is actually a greater percentage of viable oxygen produced by trees on land. However their optimum efficiency as filtering agents is directly dependant upon the plants which grow on the surface of the oceans. This mostly encompasses kelp. Kelp growth has greatly diminished. It's quantity is only two thirds of optimum normal quantity. Therefore the existing kelp and other ocean plants are reduced by one third their best efficiency. The efficiency of the land filters is decreased by one sixth. The quantity of trees have been reduced by one sixth their optimum number and efficiency. This is in direct ratio to the lessening of the remaining kelp's efficiency.

It seems there is an amplification factor to symbiotic relationships. The kelp seems to be more effective in terms of capacity than trees. Is that correct?

The trees offer higher percentage as effective filtering agents in addition to producing oxygen. Kelp produces more direct oxygen, but the efficiency of the trees to filter existing atmospheric impurities depends upon kelp and the efficiency of kelp function.

Then the two are connected to one another. If one was to analyze it scientifically, one can not treat the whole of the trees and the whole of the kelp independently within the system. The interaction

between the two must be acknowledged in order to understand the whole.
>   Correct.

You were going to add something.
>   We wish to clarify.   The existing trees filtering efficiency is reduced by one sixth because the kelp is only functioning at two thirds capacity for there are fewer trees and less kelp.

I am sure an expert scientist in the biology and biochemistry of these systems would probably have a hundred more questions for you.
>   It will set some eyes spinning.   It will provide avenues of thought for others.   That is what you are wanting to do.

You referred to humans as Terrans.   What does that mean?
>   It means you are terrestials, land functioners.   Terra is another term for Earth or land.

>   In closing we wish to offer you this.   It is quite stretching to distill a workable prescription for action when so many variants must be considered, cultures, language differences, and immediate economic conditions in different countries on this planet.   However there are methods to resolve these environmental crises that a majority of these cultures and societies have potential to agree on.   So, Dear Ones, do not become discouraged.   The potential for a Positive resolution continues.

Tao Song.

THE OCEANS AND THE CETACEANS

We have been talking about trees and what is going on on the surface of the planet. What is going on in the ocean?

This is a large, large area to consider. The most important thing to understand is this: **The ocean is not a place to put things that you do not know where to put or want to put on land!**

Like nuclear waste and garbage sludge.

Exactly. There is much damage occurring in the oceans because it is being used as a dumping ground.

How are the whales faring?

The whales are accomplishing their choices for learning on this Mother planet. Communication is being considered between whales and humans.

What are they trying to communicate to us?

The whales' choice is to make humans aware that they are not the only consciously aware, ensouled, thinking species. The whales are accomplishing this. There is great concern now for whales. Because of this concern, they are recovering some of their numbers. Further specific communication with humans is the Cetacean's choice. Whales are concerned with levels of thinking which humans would find quite stretching - difficult to relate to. They are in many ways much wiser than humans. However, it is quite possible that there will be communication between your species on a more direct basis. It depends on the free will choices of the Cetaceans.

Can they learn our language?

Cetaceans do not have the physiological vocal organs which allow them to articulate human speech. However computer technology could be designed so whales could communicate using your language in an altered form.

Because of their sonar ranging capabilities they probably have a three dimensional way of understanding and translating their thoughts into language. They can see into the interior of things with sound waves.

And the concepts and thought processes oriented to that ability would be quite disorienting to humans at times.

Would you speak about the ocean environment next?
We would be quite shardy to speak of this, yes. The Cetaceans are the monitors of the oceans. They are concerned with the condition of their environment.

What groups do Cetaceans include?
We include in that term all whales, dolphins, dugongs, and manatees.

Are they ensouled independently of one another?
Correct. They have individual Soul Patterns just as humans do.

So whales reincarnate as whales and dolphins reincarnate as dolphins?
Correct. They are people; ocean people.

Do they function at the same Rate as each other and ourselves?
They are Physical Plane functioners, yes. They have a much greater awareness of Non-physical Plane connections than most humans, in proportion to their numbers. Those old whales know what is going on. They are old practitioners of Mind Mechanics.

Why would the whales care what we think about them?
It is not that they care what you think about them. It is that they understand the need to ensure that this Mother is saved.

They have already made the Jump to Mind Mechanics, the whales.
In many aspects, yes.

So they understand the big picture, what is happening to the planet.
Also, they understand that Terrans, land people, are essential to whale function. The species agreement is that the land Enedswr, the ensouled species of the land, will be the Jump precipitators.

Humans must initiate and accomplish the Jump[31] for all species

---

[31]Jump - See the chapter "The Jump to Mind Mechanics".

and the Planet?
Correct.

How does whale thinking differ from ours?
In matters which ensure the continuation of the species, there is more flexibility in the conceptual aspect of their intellect. They have the ability to image and project spherical thought processes. We have been asked to say that they think in holograms where as Terrans still think largely in linear or two dimensional perspectives.

They appear to be totally in Balance with Nature. They do not have any visible technology. Is that correct or is it just that it is not apparent?
Whales have no material technology, correct.

Why do mass strandings of small whales occur?
Many smaller whales species have much greater exposure to ocean waters which are close to land. These coastal waters have a much higher concentration of wastes, of overall toxicity. Many strandings occur when pods of smaller whales swim through currents of concentrated wastes. Some substances act like an anesthetic to the part of the whales's brain which has to do with sonar. These chemical substances also cause the depression of the whale's immune system[32]. As a result of this, a pod can become ill and develop infections. There is generally a pod director, or leader. When the leader becomes ill and spatially or magnetically disoriented and land density is confused with deep water, the pod will follow the leader and become stranded. We would wish to give the chemicals which are the perpetrators: Hydrocarbon based solvents, heavy salts from forms of detergents, and also industrial waste from hydrocarbon refineries.

When migrating across thousands of miles of open and deep water, how do the humpback whales, blue whales, etc. navigate and find

---

[32]A respected Cetacean research scientist has recently advanced a theory that the immune system depression due to an accumulation of toxins is the major cause of Cetacean disease. Certain non-natural synthetic compounds such as PCB's are highly soluble in fat and hence concentrate in Cetaceans rendering them susceptible to infection. Many Cetaceans have been found to have very high concentrations of these chemicals in their bodies.

their way to their predetermined destinations? They do not appear to have echolocation abilities and therefore cannot use the sea-floor to navigate with.

It is interesting to understand that these large old "grand-dads" of the whale people have many different ways of orienting in trans-oceanic travel. It is a large smile for us to see the term "migration" used. In any case, the larger whales have the ability to travel using water temperature readings, changes and directions in currents, and pressure and light changes. Also they know where they want to go. They are simply used to working with different recognition factors regarding direction. Also, it is quite interesting to consider that each mother bearing a new small (child) can transfer the knowledge of where and how to go, mind to mind, to her small. Larger whales have the ability to orient themselves using the planet's own electromagnetic fields. They can calculate direction using polar magnetism like a compass. It is going to be difficult to substantiate this ability through study or observation. However, there are delicate sensor bundles located within the second epidermal layer of the skin. Possibly observation and study of the nerve bundles, can reveal the many sensory orienting techniques used by large whales.

Dolphins are very intelligent. Why then, when they are surrounded by tuna nets, don't they just jump over the nets and swim away?
If a person can not see a threat it is less likely avoided. Dolphins have difficulty comprehending the threat of a flowing moving net for the simple reason that they read it like a natural part of the ocean flora. The net reads, in sonar, as any flowing seaweed would read. However, there is a way to resolve this issue. Nets could contain small echo transmitters at regular spacings. Then dolphins could comprehend that these nets are not part of the natural flora of the ocean. There is also another factor to consider.   Since dolphins have mental communications highly developed, why do they not simply tell other dolphins when drowning? Why do they not give "**stay away**" warnings? Dolphins are adolescents.   They are what you would call quite emotionally immature. Panic is the cause. Instead of "**stay away**" warnings they send frantic calls for help.

Killer whales seem to eat everything in the sea except humans. There has never been a recorded Orca attack on human beings. What is the reason for this behavior?
The choice, function, and purpose regarding the great whales

interactions with Orcas we are not allowed to explain. However, Orcas do not attack and kill Terrans, because ocean people do not eat beings with consciousness[33]. Orcas recognize that Terrans think. Orcas know that there has been and will be communication between whales and Terrans. The Orcas are not willing to limit that potential. It is necessary that this answer be vague. However, it is the best that can be done with words without risking influence.

Is this situation likely to change in the near future so that you can give more information on the Orcas?
It is difficult to speculate. It is of course up to the Orcas whether or not they wish to explain themselves.

Do they have memory like ourselves?
Whales not only have memory, they can consciously access their previous lifetimes. Whale anatomists will verify that there is a section in a whale's brain which seems to be incongruous with the rest of the brain in terms of form. It is a bulbous section. This is a highly developed time storage bank, information bank. So this prevents the whales' physical brain from being burnt out when contemplating Simultaneity. Their brains have memory accessing capability in which any given lifetime experience can be stored and then accessed singularly or simultaneously. This makes a whale's brain and a human's brain quite different. There are humans who are beginning to manifest the development of this brain change.

So we are beginning to evolve a similar structure.
Correct.

Do whales reason, do they use logic?
They are reasoning beings. Whether or not that means using logic depends upon your definition of the word "logic". They are, however, consciously aware of self, sapient.

What kind of conceptual elements compose the whales language. Do

---

[33]However, Orcas have been documented attacking and killing whales. This relationship between the Orcas and the other whales is unexplained. In terms of interaction between sapient moral species, i.e. The Fairns description of the whales, it is an apparent contradiction.

they have words like we use?

They use a vast range of complex sound vibrations and pitch. There are experts who feel that these songs are only for mating or calling purposes. Much whale language involves telathing.[34] There are highly developed call signals, however, for permission to send thoughts or enter into joint mental thought conference ... these words we are using, even as we speak, are whale song words that we attempt to translate into English. Somehow the explanation loses in the translation, literally. It is possible, however, with the assistance of your computers to translate the initial meaning of the song sounds.

Other than the obvious physical differences, how are the Cetaceans different from one another mentally...say a dolphin and a great whale?

As a general rule, in the Cetacean species the larger whales are "older". They are the sages. This does not mean smarter in terms of intellect potential, but they are more expanded - spiritual and perceptual expansion. The smartest, intellectually smartest, species of Cetaceans are the Belugas. They are the only Cetacean species with independent neck rotation, also. Most Cetaceans have a workable inter-species communication system, excepting Orcas. The interaction between Orcas and other Cetaceans is quite complex. Dolphins are quick mentally. Their intellectual capacity is great. However, their emotional maturity is somewhat lacking, in whale terms, that is.

In terms of language, intellectual capacity, what species would we be most able to relate, to talk to?

It is more practical to use medium size Cetaceans - Pilot whales, Minkes, or Belugas. Communication is also possible with some older (linear time) dolphins if there is access to them. On a mass scale the most potentially cooperative with humans would be the Belugas. Yes.

Do the Belugas and similar species have the ability to fantasize action or imagine action like we do?

They can imagine or fantasize. They can conceptualize. They also have the conscious capacity to recall past Nows.

Can they go back to the Atlantian civilization and recall the

---

[34]Telathing - using telepathy

interaction between men and whales in those times?

It is possible, yes. Not that this would be of great import, but in those times where there was direct working of humans and Cetaceans together, yes. Those remembered interactions could be related, if whale and human communication is developed further in this Now.

They might be able to provide us with guide lines on the means to establish communications?

Most initial contacts and day to day practical communications were done with civilizations which could telath adequately. The connection at that Now between humans and Cetaceans was established in that manner. Then working from telathing into sound and therefore language followed. There are some breakthroughs in human-cetacean communications occurring. The results of this will be known within the year (1992-1993).

Do Cetaceans have feelings. Do they fall in love?

There are species bonds more than individual to individual bonds. Family bonds are dominant. The concept of "falling in love", in your terms, is a human concept. Most Cetaceans are motivated by species altruism. Therefore pairing is motivated by species survival, as opposed to a one on one kind of romantic love. Babies belong to the pod, not just to the individual female. Although they do not evidence as coordinated a nursery effort, as say, elephants, there is an understanding of the importance of integral species function. It is difficult to explain. Many actions are not understood by humans because these sociological functions are performed by whales at such great distances from each other. It is generally thought that after the female calves, males are disallowed; that they do not have further supervisorial or protective function. This, in actuality, is not the case. It is just that the patrol areas can be ten or so miles. The males remain in contact and can provide perimeter patrol from five to ten miles.

How long would it take a Beluga whale to acquire a basic human vocabulary. If there were some phonetic structures established and some telepathic communication, would they learn to recognize the sounds and associate the words and meanings; a few hundred words or so? What kind of time period would be required relative to human abilities?

A working grasp of human speech can be accomplished in six to nine months providing the altered sound translation rate or frequency is viable.   In other words, formulating a word in English such as "concept" might not be possible for a Cetacean to reproduce.   If the word "concept" was translated into a viable sound pattern or sequence of musical notes which was within the ability of the Cetacean to reproduce, then the language could be learned within six months to a year.

Do they have an organized social structure?   Groups?   We have tribes, and we have governments and so forth.   Do they have analogous social structure, tribes, families, larger groups....?
There is an extensive structure in these terms.   Cetacean species are caretakers of certain ocean areas.   The areas in which a certain species of whale is found is the area of their job....their monitoring job of that specific area of the ocean.

Do they manage their environment.   Do they look after the plants and the other animals?
All species of Cetaceans are environmental managers except Orcas and Blues.   Blue whales are the great Magiis or Masters.   Orcas have a completely different function than any other of the whales species.   They are the life-crises controllers for the Cetacean species.   That is all we may give on the function of Orcas.

It seems that dolphins and whales take the extermination of their fellow species by humans with more understanding than we might, if the situation were reversed.   Can you explain that?
This is an area which gets into metaphysics.   Whales have made a pre-life agreement to teach humans.   The dolphins and whales are your teachers in this matter of respect for every species.   It is essential first for humans to understand that they are not the only thinking beings on this Mother.   In actuality, when humans kill Cetaceans, they are murdering ocean "people."   The agreement to teach Homo Sapiens that, as a thinker they are not alone, was a pre-life species choice of the Cetaceans.   Once humans learn that killing Cetaceans is killing "people", the problem will resolve itself.   Communication will, therefore, be of much greater benefit and potential.   It is being learned.   Not quickly enough for Searchers like yourself, but it is being learned.

Yesterday would be soon enough.   What is the most direct route to that learning?   Communication research?
That and the accurate assessment of Cetaceans' motives, plus

their voluntary associations directed towards humans. There is a need for humans to recognize the Cetaceans' kindness; their willingness to interact. Those two factors are greatly ignored. A collection of incidents which have documented voluntary interaction between wild Cetacean species and humans could prove quite extensive and interesting. The obvious choice to interact, and, in many instances, to be self sacrificial in order to assist humans in need should be recognized and understood exactly for what it is.

Can you give an example of that?
Dolphins saving children from drowning. Dolphins fighting sharks to prevent them attacking stranded persons. Pilot whales encircling and actually towing small boats. There are many other instances. Also some species have chosen to make contact with humans and play together. If these behaviors were documented without clinical reserve, recognized as demonstrations of intelligence and human empathy, the realization that Cetaceans are "people" would spread.

How can we assist in making humans realize that Cetaceans are "people?"
State your feelings to all who will listen. State what we have given. Say that Cetaceans are ocean "people." When one is killed, it is MURDER. Imagine carving up your next door neighbor in order to use part of shis body to make perfume last longer. Many whale products are used as scent extenders.[35]

Is there still whaling going on?
In some areas, but this is now much less. The most critical toll of Cetacean life is due to ocean trash and fishing nets. This information may not win you large smiles from fishing companies, but there is no moral reason that ocean "people" must continue to die when viable fishing methods exist to prevent that occurrence.

It is very difficult to sit by while fellow Terrans slaughter "people" in large numbers due to our own ignorance of the state of affairs. In a pragmatic sense there is only so much time in the day.
Correct. That is why boycotts can be quite effective. It would be a powerful statement if one whole town for one whole year refused

---

[35]Ambergris, which comes from whales, is used to make perfume.

to eat anything from the ocean which was secured using nets. Even an individual instituting this boycott makes a statement. That action is a Positive contribution also. It is true that sometimes the challenges are so vast and seem so overwhelming that people become discouraged and think that one person can not do much. But it is true that "every little bit helps" and the energy and conviction of the individual, the thoughts surrounding Positive action, also contribute potential for a Positive resolve. That energy helps the Mother planet also. Do not be fooled by the "Too little, too late" philosophy. Positive intent energizes Positive energy, Positive potential, and Positive action.

You mentioned that the whales are aware of our situation. What are the results of their observation of our actions?

The results are that the whales are more informed and reassured regarding the intent of humans towards their species.

What do the whales report regarding the condition of oceans?

There are two main factors which are critical. These are: Non-recyclable wastes and metal deterioration; processed metals which are deteriorating. These two factors precipitate the most immediate danger to the Mother's oceans. Much sewage is dumped into the ocean. Although this is undesirable, it is manageable. There is sufficient plant and animal life to process this organic waste. It is the non-recyclable toxic chemical wastes which are so damaging. Also, there has been extensive dumping of refined or processed metals. More than is commonly known. Much of these metals are containers, which are in a critical state of degeneration.

What is in these containers? Radioactive wastes?

Radioactive wastes, yes, but more importantly, biochemical wastes, - engineered biochemical waste. The greatest danger is that containers holding genetically engineered substances, viruses, bacteria are deteriorating to a point where these may be released into the Ocean's body.

Are you talking about germ warfare containers?

Germ containers, Yes. All were not specifically intended to be for warfare. However, there are many bio-laboratory containers which have had to be sealed off and disposed of somewhere. This is the greatest threat to all, both whales and humans - all life - if those canisters deteriorate beyond salvage. The most Positive intent for

Human-Whale interaction at this Now is to locate and retrieve these canisters so that the contents can be isolated. The whales are not despondent regarding the threat to the oceans. They are greatly alarmed, but they also see that this situation is a further opportunity to establish communication with Terrans. Then cooperative maintenance methods can be established. These canisters and substances can be monitored and retrieved or repaired when needed. That is one of the goals of the Cetaceans. It is the only responsible way to interact to ensure Positive and safety for all.

Back in the nineteen fifties there were hundreds or thousands of radioactive waste canisters dumped off the Farlon Islands.
Correct.

Those are the containers that are leaking and contaminating the California coast? Is the general populace unaware of this?
There are many other storage containers which are reaching critical stages, also. But, there are steps being taken to rectify this. The work, of course, is, as you have stated, under cover. In a pragmatic sense this makes no difference. It is being done. The important factor is to develop methods to coordinate these efforts with the Cetaceans. They know the exact locations of the dump sites. As you have felt rightly, the only way to do this is to have open knowledge of quantities and condition of the canisters so that immediate organized action may be taken by people who understand proper handling procedures. Of course, people who are most learned in Cetacean-Human communications would be essential to the work.

The germ canisters need to be located, also, and then we need to do something about them?
This is why the whales are working on communications as a priority. The first whales to be emissaries most likely will be gray whales for they are oriented towards interaction. The whales can assist in finding and reporting the location, quantity, and condition of the canisters.

Last week we chartered a boat and went out to where the Gray whales are migrating. We were hoping to be able to establish and document, via video camera, some communications. Would you please explain the whales decision not to support our attempt to document communications between us?

It was a last minute change of plans involving a combination of factors which were occurring at that Now. The whales knew you were there before you knew they were there. The two who started to come in your direction where ordered not to make obvious interaction. This decision was a majority decision, but the totality of members were not in total accord as to the change of plans. We were not successful in our attempts to persuade the majority to allow interactions. The basis of the decision was as follows:

It was felt that even with documentation or video that the evidence would not be considered significant. There was also the possibility that distribution of that video accounting would cause great numbers of people to come to the area in an attempt to accomplish similar contacts. Based upon former direct communication attempts by the ocean peoples, it was decided that these would be potential contacts with the wrong intent. Each time, former attempts have been incorrectly interpreted as simply a behavior response.

We interjected our willingness to act as direct translator which we, of course, had discussed with the ocean people previously. However, we have no will to coerce any peoples. Therefore, when the change of mind occurred, we would not interfere. We requested a commitment for future attempts and were told that it will be considered. The thought processes of Terrans and ocean people are so different that it is complex to understand direct communications even when they are made. When we suggested that even one small, you might say, parlor trick by the ocean people could be of direct significance the majority were somewhat insulted, asking in return whether or not this would only uphold the Terran belief that certain stimulus produce certain behavioral responses. In other words our suggestion was vetoed.

Unless there is a willingness by Cetaceans to cooperate in making their abilities known, any attempt on our part will be insupportable. We would then appear, in the view of many Cetacean researchers, to be misinformed. Is there desire on the Cetaceans part to have humans generally aware of their "people" nature?

It is an issue which is hotly debated among groups of ocean people still. There is also some uncertainty as to Terrans altruistic intent at times. Some ocean people still feel Terrans might snatch several individuals and place them in confinement in order to perfect communication techniques. We are speaking of the larger whales. It is difficult, even for a volunteer whale, because larger species tend to sicken when kept in confined spaces.

If there is a desire to make humans aware of the Cetacean's nature in the future, what are the Cetacean's plans for accomplishing this?

It is difficult to speculate in terms of futures. It is as risky for us to speculate on the ocean peoples decisions or choices as it is to interfere with Terrans choices.

Is it necessary for Humans and Cetaceans to work together to accomplish our goals?

It is necessary. It is occurring. More and more Terrans are believing ocean people are sapient whether or not there is proof from the "scientific community". However, there are large complexities. In order to accomplish some goals, the scientific community must be convinced. This problem, the recovery and locations of the canisters we spoke of previously, is still being debated.

What happens to Cetaceans during a polar shift? Do they survive well or are they nearly exterminated?

It is dependant upon location. However, there has been large decimation in some previous shifts. Your observation regarding Cetaceans being somewhat at the mercy of Terrans' creations is correct.

How do we facilitate establishing communication through a common language?

It is possible to bring these factors to the attention of scientists and people who study Cetaceans. Also, support any individual's technology which might prevent the need for further dumping of waste canisters. There are technologies being developed which neutralize the harmful chemicals and microbes before storage is necessary. You are already aware of this kind technology. For example, the biogest[36] project.

Can we define the scope of the problem in the ocean to some extent - magnitude, canisters? It must be world wide. Let's start with that.

There are over three million, fifty gallon canisters. There are nearly one million, five hundred gallon canisters. There are five hundred thousand nuclear bars in containers. This is in the Pacific ocean alone.

---

[36]Biogest - A technology in which micro organisms consume toxic waste rendering it inert.

There are more in the other oceans?
    Correct.   The most workable method is to consolidate all
containers within an area which can be maintained and monitored
carefully. It is possible to construct several such installations which
could be safely maintained.

In the ocean?
    Yes.   Safe monitoring methods and non-degenerative storage
materials could be used to manage these dangerous substances. Storing
these in the ocean does have one advantage until your technology
develops neutralizing processes. This advantage is the water pressure.
The pressure can keep the contents of the waste canisters more stable
than they would be on land, providing these wastes are placed in
containers made of materials which do not deteriorate.   It is also
essential to have these canisters in locations where monitoring and
maintenance are constant. The help that the Cetaceans can give with
this is immeasurable.

**That sounds like a task for a government. It is a large task in terms
of organized governmental effort.**
    Correct.

**Is there any time frame under which we are working to avoid major
disasters?**
    There are some alternate experiments being undertaken by other
ocean dwellers. They are working to develop an alternate material - a
silicate crystalline growth which could adhere to the surface of the metal
canisters.   Their consensus is that the critical stages for metal
deterioration is forty-five to seventy-five years.

**What kind of thing is it, that lives in a container and can be released
and cause so much damage?**
    Some contain gene altering compounds. Containers holding
these substances are the most unreliable.

Are we still producing that type of thing and putting it in the water?
    There is much research into gene plasma alteration occurring.
Yes.

**Can you expand on that?   What kinds of compounds are being
developed?**

There are many genetic engineering experiments with DNA/ RNA cycles. Some of these projects can produce errors which reach uncontrollable and erratic growth rates. It is difficult to be specific. Some developments have been failures, some have been disasters. Mostly, the intent is to develop Positive function for these experiments. However, without more care in monitoring, the results can be frightening and disastrous. It is important for all to understand that this kind of research can be quite beneficial and quite Positive. It is essential however to get the research out of the "secret" status and have no military interests backing the research. This may be too touchy to include in the book. It is given, however, for intense consideration.

Can you continue with the discussion of germ containers being put into the ocean? Particularly we want to define the problem and arrest it at its current state.

We would offer this: Develop technology which can effectively neutralize these compounds **before** dumping or storage measures are needed.

What kind of process would neutralize these wastes?

Carefully isolated systems within a vacuum. Filtering processes incorporating natural enzymes are most effective. With certain germ forms, a vacuum environment must be observed. It is possible to develop a series of organic processing agents which eventually convert or neutralize all stages of the waste breakdown. The result will then be recyclable organic base material or inert mineral wastes which could be plowed into the soil as fertilizer or returned directly to the environment for reabsorption. There are some prototype waste processors of this kind being developed at this Now. We feel that the important factor is to release the knowledge that these experiments and researches are going on. Make this knowledge available to the general public so that a broader system of checks and balances can be initiated. It is difficult to monitor a process or project if people do not know that the project is occurring. Freedom of information!

Maybe we could shed some light on where the research is taking place. Is it primarily governmental or is it primarily private industry?

Most are private industries. Three of the largest projects involving genetic development are supported by private industry. At times using the word "private" is vague because many of the private industry interests lead directly to defense organizations. And in many cases because they are "private," the care in monitoring waste material is not subject to as many outside checks and balances.

I am sure this genetic research is a complex area that covers a broad spectrum.

Correct. There are some extensive research projects whose purpose is to genetically amplify viruses. For instance, viruses which can be engineered to attack specific species or organisms. This is one such kind of research. Another is viruses which attack certain materials, such as rubber and plastics.

One could see how that could be dangerous if specific viruses for humans or whales were developed.

Trees!

A mutant virus that would destroy the trees?

What do you think a defoliant is? There are not only chemical defoliants.

Biological defoliants? Active viruses?

Correct. The intent behind most of this research is to create factors which strengthen the natural resistance of trees to disease. What is over looked, in developing the intended Positive result, is that attempts which are unsuccessful have to be dumped somewhere. All the failures - all the laboratory cultures which do not result in the desired end product - have to, literally, be trashed somewhere. If these combine with other research project garbage, the combination can create unfathomable problems. It is not an objection to the actual research itself that we are making. We are offering this consideration: that all waste, especially in this kind of research must be monitored and carefully, but CAREFULLY processed. It is frightening to think how many test tube or petri dish contents have actually gone down the sewer drain.

How critical is the situation in the oceans with respect to the pollution?

It is approaching a critical level. It has not progressed beyond the "point of no return" but once critical level is reached, the "point of no return" can come very quickly. In actuality there can be no "point of no return", for other forces will engage to ensure that this point is not reached. However the critical point can occur as soon as thirty years, even twenty five years, if unmonitored, unrecycled or unprocessable waste products continue to be dumped into the oceans.

You talked about the germ canisters, what are some of the other wastes you are talking about?

There are mercury canisters that are leaking badly. There are huge quantities of old armaments which are degenerating and the combination of ocean water and sulfur[37] produce heavy salts.

Heavy metal salts?

Correct. These metals: shells, large bullets, should be retrieved. Metal ships wherever possible should be retrieved from the water. This is feasible. Possibly, costly, but it is feasible. There are also large quantities of dilute acids. These are not as difficult for sea life and ocean conditions to process, but the time required for processing these acids adds to the rapidity at which the metal casings are deteriorating. There are many factors to consider. We could more beneficially approach this from the reverse direction. If all hard chemical wastes would be outlawed and all ocean dumping halted for one year, most of the major irregularities in water quality could be resolved. The result would add twenty five years, yes, <u>twenty-five years</u>, within which to retrieve those deteriorating metal containers. Yes.

Is this concentrated in certain areas?

This is where Cetaceans and humans can inter-act most effectively. There are areas of concentration, but there are quantities which have strayed and could be difficult to discover with sonar or metal detecting devices. Ocean bottom storms can also be a factor in this. This is where whales can be of great assistance.

What do you mean by ocean storms?

Every surface storm is reflected by equal turbulence on the ocean floor. When there is a large hurricane there is an ocean bottom storm simultaneously. Storms move with as great intensity on the bottom of the oceans as they do on the surface. That is what we are meaning by ocean bottom storms. Sometimes ocean current deviation

---

[37]Many explosives contain large quantities of sulfur.

can cause a bottom storm which will assist the development of a surface storm.

Are there more areas to discuss with regards to the ocean?

You might ask yourselves this question: Would people like to contend with taking a bath, shower, or drinking water which contains solvents, or acids, and mercury salts - to the point where even the smell is noxious?   That is what humans are accomplishing for ocean inhabitants.

If it was up to us - and it is not, unfortunately - we would take the necessary steps to put a stop to this, immediately. Or as soon as possible.

And you are doing that very thing. One can only take action within ones own individual sphere of control and territory. You are doing all that is in your control to make this better.

The key is to put the focus of comment or stress not on what is occurring, but on Positive individual action - careful processing of waste and waste by products from research projects. That action will insure both individual safety and ocean safety. The main thrust should be to properly monitor products and by-products of on going research projects.

Oil spills are much publicized examples of major damage to the oceans and coastal life. Is this a big problem and, if it is, what can we do about it?

This has been a large problem. There has been a recent disaster, within the last week, a very large spill in the Gulf of Mexico. Engineered strains of processing bacteria have been introduced to consume the oil. From what we have observed, this is functioning quite effectively. There does not seem to be any mutation occurring and the bacteria become glomerate. They become glomerate and are easily swept from the surface after the oil has been consumed. So in terms of oil spills this new development looks very promising. Of course there is still a great amount of damage from previous accidents. In some places, it is still quite detrimental, not to mention upsetting.

Can this new method using the bacteria be used on old spills?

It is an issue which is being considered. The main complication or problem is that once the slick crude oil has been exposed to oxygen, over a period of time, oxidation occurs and the tar state is reached. This is much more difficult to deal with, especially when spills are in colder climates. However this technological development using a specialized bacteria looks very promising.

Do you have anything more to say about the oil spill damage and clean up?

There is not nearly enough use being made of recycled foam to assist with these accidents. There are large quantities of the material you call "pop corn"; styrofoam designed for packing material. If large quantities of granulated styrofoam were dumped into the area of a spill in a circular pattern, to surround the spill; then air blown currents to compress and corral the slick, the oil would readily adhere to the foam. Then it could easily be netted or vacuumed up. This has not been considered. It has not been thought of.[38]

Could this quantity of ground up styrofoam be included on the oil rigs themselves?

You have hit up upon vast idea!

What other aspects of the ocean do you wish to discuss?

We did not get into which substances are causing damage to the oceans.

We wish to state that unprocessed sewage is in some areas a great detriment. Also detergent. Detergent is one of the factors that imbalances quantity of algae. It is not so much that algae itself is detrimental, it is the detergents which upset the quantity Balance. We can state there are very effective water wetting compounds which can replace all types of phosphate detergents. They have been available for twenty five years.

Detergent is one of the elements in the sewage.

Phosphates are also a great hazard. It is important to understand that the issue is not only what is being dumped, but the **quantity** which is crucial. The ocean's system can process these compounds, but not in

---

[38]This particular combination is unique. However, using styrofoam to absorb spilled oil is included in several patents in patent class 210/693. See Horowitz, #3494862, 2/70; Wienberg, #3756948, 9/73; Winkler, #3929631, 12/75; Sugimori, et al, #4801386, 1/89. Winkler proposes using waste styrofoam combined with other meltable hydro carbons to clean up ocean oil spills.

the **quantity** they are being forced to deal with.

Are the Oceans completely overloaded?
Not to the point of "no return," as we have stated before. But this is why the attempt to achieve Balance is so crucial. The more trees that are eradicated the less chance the oceans' systems have to process what they are being asked to process.

The connection between the trees and the kelp we spoke of before?
Correct.

We may have already asked this question but I will ask it again. What are the most significant factors causing damage to the oceans?

The trees being eliminated, chemicals, and radioactive dumping. The trees are the most important factor, however.

Would you like to make any more comments in this area?
We will send a shardy poke to all: **Do not dump waste without adequate knowledge of the processes and time required to convert what is dumped.** That is the rule to follow.

What is it in the ocean that processes the waste?
The living organic system itself. The organisms which begin the living food chain are the most important. Many wastes are processed by the smallest organisms in the ocean; the least complex cellularly. The plankton, algaes, kelp forests. They are the organisms which initiate the primary steps of processing. These are the organisms which can make the dumped materials palatable again for the subsequent links in the cycle. If these primary organisms are overloaded with excessive quantities of toxic waste, then toxins become cumulative as they move along the food chain. Eventually a higher member of the food chain becomes irretrievably contaminated and the chain is broken. This toxic process can kill the entire working system of the ocean. Therefore, generate thought and action which supports neutralization before dumping is necessary.

Tao Song.

TECHNOLOGY

Let's talk about the philosophy and products of our technology.
With respect we wish to ask: Do you know that there is enough metal already mined and available for use to meet the needs of every person on this planet forever?   As long as the population numbers remain constant for this Mother, you never have to mine more ore. Recycling what is already refined. Do you see?

The most Beneficial attitude change is "Recycle" - and this is not only in garbage. Think of the recycling process of any material which occurs within any living system. Think on the concept of "Being Recycling."

When we talked about recycling before, you mentioned a balloon effect. Could we discuss that further? Explain the balloon effect to us.
Which aspect of the balloon effect in terms of recycling did you wish to reopen.

You indicated that recycling in nature's systems not only reuses the material over and over again so that it is not lost, but another factor operates that produces a net gain. So in each step in the process of recycling, something more than what is in the system is created, thereby expanding the whole system. You presented this in an esoteric way. We could benefit by a more concrete example.
Within celestial bodies, planets and stars there is a measurable continuous expansion. Suns enlarge as they age, radiating energy outward. This is measurable energy expanding outward. Also, habitable and inhabited planets with the living features of those planets do the same through the cycles of the life processes operating on those planets. The energies, in terms of measurable atmospheric chemicals or gases, are constantly pressing outward.   When all systems are ecologically Balanced on a planet, the atmospheric envelope tends to extend itself continuously. This is measurable. This is the "Greater Reality" of the process of **Recycling**. The basis of continuous creation is the process of generating more recyclable energy.   It is somewhat difficult to delineate in linear terms.   The expanding creative energy becomes material, recyclable matter and then increases itself. It is the "action" energy within the process of the **Recycling** which creates more and

therefore creates continual expansion. Your science and technology will be capable of measuring this process, someday.

Perhaps we can get in to the subject of Recycling in terms of the things people use.   One of the things that we can do to assist recycling of material is to make things that last longer.

We send you a large smile. There is, soon in-coming,[39] a new development by a team; two persons we have watched.   One is a physicist and the other is a chemical engineer. In this team there are also several metal consultant experts. This team is working on plasteel. There is a good possibility that they will develop a workable product within ten to fifteen years.

No new resources will be needed to make plasteel.   Those metals already mined and plastics which are already made can be converted to the new material. This substance, which has many variants and is used in many other worlds, is quite durable. It is also easily reshaped. This one break through will greatly assist in many of your recycling problems. All forms of plasteel can be reused again and again.

Is there anything we can do to assist in the development of that material?

Continue to be aware of day to day resource conservation. You are already contributing essentials on your own parts.

Is plasteel very strong? Is it as strong as steel?

It is as strong as steel and has the added ability of being flexible. It has a greater tensile strength. It can be reformed and reused without damage to its molecular structure and thus its tensile strength.

Is it reformed with a heating process?

It is pressure molded using sound vibrations to accomplish restructure. No heat is required because it is pressure malleable. If it is used within a human body for a joint or a skeletal correction it is completely adaptable and inert. Used for medical purposes it does not trigger the human bodies' rejection system.   There is no potential toxicity through degeneration. If it is buried in the Earth it is totally inert.

---

[39]In-coming - a future development, not yet in existence.

There is a biological recycling system under development locally for recycling human waste in a garden.

That is a viable concept. Also, human wastes can be used to produce methane which is relatively clean burning. Methane is a viable "transition" fuel. It is possible to use methane to initiate a self contained system: methane to power a compressor which compresses methane that can be used for automobiles. Very little alteration of carburetion and exhaust system would be needed in order to use this type of compressed gas.

We wish to offer you this. There is a process which is already being used in public transportation. Busses in Germany, Austria, and some parts of France already have this system. This is not a methane system, but it is a self-contained fuel system. Although we are digressing, the concept of self-containment which is being developed is a large breakthrough in itself.

Could you explain self-containment?

A system that uses it own waste to create a useable product in sufficient quantities required to power the same system; therefore no ecologically incompatible by-products occur through exhaust.

There is a system of gardening designed so nothing has to be brought into the garden to keep it producing.

Exactly. It is the application of the concept of "perpetual motion." Humans excrete, the same as animals, trees, and all living things. It is viable to use this as a resource. This is one aspect of recycling: Using waste to produce a resource.

This leads us back to technology. You mentioned clean energy previously. Let's talk about clean energy.

Solar is the most effective potential for Balance. However, it can also be the most danger fraught, for it is limitless.

Would you explain the reasoning behind that statement?

Solar energy is clean and efficient. For practical purposes it is available in unlimited quantities. However, the secondary technologies harnessing solar energy can become dangerous. Solar energy harnessed in large quantities through machines or devices and used for self aggrandizement - Negative purposes - can create much Negative. Solar energy for powering livingry[40] is the most perfect Balance.   Solar energy, if used for weaponry, can be intensely dangerous and Negative. Therefore, the use of solar energy is completely dependant on the **intent** of those who use it. Fossil fuels create detrimental residue. Fossil fuels used for livingry or weaponry leave detrimental residue. This is not the case with solar. Solar energy is completely non-polluting. Therefore the only danger is tied to the **intent** behind its use and the intensity with which it is used.

If solar energy is non-polluting, what is the difference between using solar energy to charge a battery system for a House and using solar energy for the guidance system of a military missile?

It is not the energy itself which is polluting. However, Negative energy can be created if the **intent** of the person using **any** source of energy is Negative - harmful to living systems. Thought energy motivated by Negative intent brings potential cataclysm much more rapidly.

So the thought energy is amplified when solar is used.

No, the energy created by an individual's intent and thoughts is absorbed into the aura energy of the planet as opposed to the Physical matter energy of the planet. Physics. It is physics verses metaphysics in this instance. We will present a tangible example. Suppose solar energy was used by those of perverted intent - to make a laser, for example - so powerful that it could sear the Mother to shis core. A weapon such as this was invented by a past civilization on this Mother planet.

A previous civilization invented a laser beam so powerful that it nearly shot through the earth?

Correct. Using solar powered devices which focused direct sunlight beams.

Going out into space; a space to ground laser?

Not exactly. Previous civilizations had crystals which, when programmed and placed in direct sunlight, could focus solar power of laser intensity and capability, Yes.

---

[40]   Ibid, Fuller.

No doubt you would not mention this if it was not pertinent.

It is especially important when using solar energy not to assume that exploitation, for purposes of greed, is acceptable, simply because solar energy is non-polluting. Do not overlook the long term effects of indiscriminate use of solar. It is necessary to be prudent regarding how it is used and what it is used for. There must be clear intention that the use of solar energy not be for developing imbalance with the planet and shis living systems. Many civilizations have been lost because they thought that since solar energy is clean, other factors, such as "intent", need not be considered. Many civilizations were excessive in the quantity and intent of solar use. Solar energy is an energy source which can free a civilization to advance technologically with such efficiency and rapidity that, often, what occurs is fascination and romance with the advanced technology. Then the growth of technology overbalances the desire to keep spiritual growth at the same level. Then ensues a loss of purpose, a confusion of purpose. Then this Mother's plan of "The Individual in Balance with Technology and Enlightenment" is lost. Technological civilizations have a tendency to "fall in love" with their toys.

We are wanting to make very clear that we are not stating to avoid the use of solar energy as a means to resolve your energy crises, pollution crises, and technological crises. We would, by all means, state that this avenue is the most Positive and effective in order to clean up fossil fuel residues. It is important, however, to have large, loud reminders that solar is not the Be All and End All. It does not ensure that because all will be well fed, well clothed, well housed, and have much time for leisure and luxuries, that this is the only thing life is.

Through solar technology we can achieve a global high standard of living for everyone.

Quite. Yes.

The current situation with regards to solar electric converters is that commercial solar electric converters are not very efficient; getting only 11 percent efficiency.

We wish to call something to mind here. It is not only the light which you are trying to save. We are speaking of more efficient ways of storing solar energy, more than using batteries. The important thing in increasing solar battery efficiency is to not forget that you want to save the heat also. Not a battery which saves the actual heat, but developing a jacket for the cell which is enhanced by solar heat. It is,

most probably, a confusing hint at best.
Do you wish to speak of fusion?

You have mentioned that lightning is cold fusion. Is it a process that can be used for power generation and is it Positive for the environment?
It is.

It would not be surprising to find most scientists chuckle at the idea of lightning being cold fusion.
And what is it generally thought that it is?

Good question. Perhaps a plasma arc.
And what is this besides fusion?

That is what we need to ask you. How that process works.
The cold fusion process occurs. The result which you see as lightning is the by-product. Lightning is what the cold fusion process makes. The process requires natural environmental conditions. In specific atmospheric conditions certain temperatures, friction in air masses, and rates (speeds) of matter excite the free hydrogen atoms to produce photonums. When these storm conditions reach a critical mass they arc into lightning. But the lightning itself is only the by product of cold fusion.

What is a photonum?
It is a particle which is produced in the process. It is a particle, but it is also the process/state/by-product which is produced when light, sound, and temperature come together under certain conditions to allow free hydrogen atoms to fuse. This melding produces the birth of photonums which then arc off as lightning.

So it is a combination of the correct temperature, vibrations, and some light?
And, of course, it is important to consider the magnetism that those three factors draw. The friction creates the magnetism which is the actual beginning of the process.

Can we lay this out in a time sequence? We have available some free hydrogen in the clouds someplace.
Correct. All atmosphere has some quantity of free hydrogen.

A positively charged cloud, if you like. Free hydrogen ions which are just protons.
Correct.

And these protons somehow interact and fuse into a heavy hydrogen, or helium nucleus, a proton becomes a neutron. So that is the fusion process.
Correct.

One can create free protons, the trick is to get the fusion. So there is something in the process which is escaping us. Putting protons in the vicinity of each other does not create fusion. You have to slam them together.
Or create a correct environment in which they can **voluntarily** meld. It is not necessary to slam them together. Under the right environmental conditions, they will voluntarily meld. The offspring, photonums, being the collective particle state which manifests as lightning. It is a truth in reality. Proof for credibility of the concept is another matter altogether.

Right. That could be a challenge. Doesn't fusion give off gamma radiation? So one can observe fusion in terms of lightning just by monitoring gamma radiation. Is this possibly correct?
Correct. It is quite possible. This radiation is a part of ozone.

Lightning creates ozone.
Yes. We wish to offer this. It is detectable just before and after a lightning bolt.

Great. That makes it very easy to trace. A burst on a gamma detector followed by lightning flash.
Or more like an in drawn breath, a rapid but steady increase in radiation; then the lightning arc.

We can produce lightning arcs in the laboratory from a charged sphere across an air gap to a grounded conductor. Is this also a cold fusion process?
It still requires input of energy to build up in order to have laboratory lightning. Although what you see at the instant the lightning seems to be a possible form of cold fusion, it is not cold fusion in that

sense, because external energy is required to produce lightning in the laboratory. Natural environmental conditions leading to a release of lightning constitute true cold fusion.

Let me ask you a verification of the definition of fusion.
Fusion is a proton converted to a neutron.... two hydrogen ions forming a heavy hydrogen nucleus.
Correct, and the resulting offspring of that union is a new particle which has not as yet been observed, other than in its collective state as lightning.

What are the properties of the new particle? Does it have a spin?
On dispersing from their collective state, photonums go directly to Stress Ether function, they escape measurable Physical function. That which stays is the particle of which you spoke previously (gamma).

The photonum is not directly observable.
Correct. Other than in the collective state.

This is complicated.
It is quite complex. Yes.

The concept is difficult. However, picking the right avenues for research is what creates great advances. Research can be done in many directions. If it is taken sequentially only, answers would often never be found. The path to investigate has to be guessed sometimes.
Based on what I know, I do not see anything wrong with the idea. It is another matter to make the necessary measurements to expand the understanding and then expand on to applications.
The correct expansion can be quite lengthy, yes.

One of the reasons lightning was brought up is that you mentioned it is cold fusion. Most would consider that unlikely based on what is currently known. We want to continue, so the people who look at this concept with some interest and real knowledge have a little more substantial information to work with. It is important that we verify the things that you tell us as much as we can. We then have confidence in those things you tell us which we can not verify.
We wish to give a thing for thought. When science goes outside of phenomena available in Nature they are pursuing dead end

streets. The concept of cold fusion is valid. Fusion occurring in Nature is a reality. You have all experienced lightning. To force fusion in artificial settings will only mean that fusion will continue to elude practical methods along those lines of pursuit. Therefore, if an example of fusion which occurs in Nature can be given, this hurdle of categorical dismissal could be surmounted much more easily. This is the error of thought: Scientists do not believe that fusion occurs in Nature; readily in Nature. We are simply wanting to offer the fact that fusion **does** readily occur in Nature. If scientists spend as much time observing and studying the natural actuality as they, most probably, will spend attempting to deny that actuality, the keys to fusion could be opening practical doors in five to ten years[41].

That would be wonderful. Some people will be very excited about that. Is there anything else you would like to say about fusion before we leave it?
No. Proceed.

Let's change directions. How does one prod the development of technology in the Positive direction?
By doing that which you are doing this Now moment. Every thought, every excitation, every joy feeling is a contribution to the Positive pole.   Continue to do so.   Each person that you share enlightenment with, in joy, will share with two others who will share with two others. It is belief in the reality, say of cold fusion, which will change technology and scientists more quickly.

Wonderful. What level of technology is required to make The Jump to Mind Mechanics?
It will not be long.   The degree of technological growth is advancing at an immense pace. The spiritual awareness is engaged also and is catching up rapidly. It is impossible to gradate a certain degree of advanced technology. Some technology which seems primitive to you

---

[41]The current primary approach to fusion is based on the process occurring in the sun. Creating and containing that process is difficult due to the high temperatures and pressures required. In a lightning process, one can speculate that charged particles are released, becoming free charge, as part of the fusion process. This in turn could increase the voltage potential initiating the lightning arc.

at this Now, other civilizations would find exceptional. Even the Lemuran civilization would be amazed at some of your technology.

The focus of desire to accomplish The Jump put to day-to-day action. Not forced or done anxiously. For example, a person who wished, more than anything, to learn telepathy and practices six hours a day until shis is so frazzled that shis collapses, can not learn more quickly. It is the person who wishes to learn and practices with laughter and joy, stopping as soon as the joy feelings are gone or the person is tired; this is the person who learns more quickly. It is knowing also, that these things are inherent human abilities that only must be remembered; reawakened.

In these days of potential for global peace most of the natural resources, possibly the majority of money assigned to research and development, goes into weapons systems. What can be done to create Positive channels for this energy?

You will find within two to three years[42] there will occur a global focus switch to "livingry[43]" as opposed to weaponry. It is a group Soul Pattern decision. It is already occurring. Within the last six months, there have been very evident manifestations of the intent to convert to livingry as opposed to weaponry.   As we are reading cumulative potentials and the decisions of individuals, this will and does continue.

That is the best news I have heard in decades. Wonderful.

It is so very smiley for us also. You might say the spheres are singing.

Yesterday you were very excited about a combination earth steel construction technology.

Through compaction of soil reinforced by mesh or net.

And you can use that for walls?

And ceilings. A natural binder can be included to complete the sound yet harmonious material.

---

[42]Given in 1990.

[43] ibid, R. Buckminster Fuller

Is this available technology?
    Yes, there is a viable earth compaction process for building[44] which can save trees.
    It is interesting that humans admire the small insect species called bee so greatly and yet make such little use of the potential building designs based on the structures that bees build. Bees build the most architecturally sound and space saving structure of any builder on this Mother. It is possible to use that bee hive structure, the interlocking hexagon chamber in any size. Using that design, it is possible to build skyscrapers using viable materials and have the construction be element resistant - structurally sound in terms of an earthquake or storm.

Offshore drilling for oil and offshore production of oil is a controversial area. Is this damaging to the environment in a big way?
    There is great risk when water is used to replace oil withdrawn from the subsurface strata. The pressure and viscosity are completely different between oil and water. The inner crust reacts to difference substance changes. There is great potential to create volatile gas combinations. All in all, we would say, Yes. It is not only harmful but quite dangerous.

To surface species?
    Correct. And dangerous to the Mother's inner core displacement and crust stability.

In a global or a local sense?
    It can be both of course, depending upon quantity of water used and the square area of infusion.

Is the temperature a factor in that?
    Temperature is the factor that can increase the potential for volatile gas formation. Fossil fuels are resources which are most efficient when used for purposes other than propulsion or power.

What other forms would that be?
    Not used for energy. Used for other product production.

---

[44] Two California companies using compaction technology are Earth Home and Rammed Earth Works.

Plastics?

Correct, also fabrics. There is also in-coming an important role for crude oil in the construction of plasteel and plas-ceramic superconductors. When crude oil is burned for fuel this prevents the resource being used in technology to clean up the mess that burning crude oil created. This is a wordy way of saying "No fossil materials for fuel."

Most of the oil goes for energy, for vehicles, and things like that.

And electricity.

Electricity can be converted. We can go to natural gas, but that is a fossil fuel. So that is not a Positive. No doubt you understand the situation. Solar is the most advantageous but it does not look like it is happening in a major way for utilities. What is holding it back?

Stockpiled, hidden under the rug solar technology, patents[45]. Effective solar technology has already been developed and to a degree of great efficiency. It is the existing greed factor surrounding oil which must be dealt with and you understand this.

Of course. So the technology is already there to produce what, inexpensive and efficient solar cells, and storage systems?

Many companies buy technology already developed so that these cannot be used.

What can we do to loosen up the strings on the technology so that it can come on line?

The question you are raising with this material is potentially quite effective.

It is very frustrating at times being pragmatic, waiting.....

Yes, but by stating there is solar technology already available will encourage many people to start scratching their heads and asking

---

[45] There are several hundred U.S. patents on photoelectric conversion processes. One interesting concept is a thermo-photovoltaic approach. In this process the suns rays heat a thermal radiator. Low voltage bandgap semiconductor cells then convert radiant heat emitted from the radiator to electricity. The advantage is the ability of the device to process the full spectrum of light energy.

questions. It may seem like lighting a fire under a seated mule, but one small fuse is all you need if you have dynamite.

What kind of advances are we talking about here? What are the technologies which have been shelved?
One is a solar conversion process which does not require cells for storage. We will only state it is a direct process. It requires fewer conversion steps and therefore the efficiency is much greater.

How much greater?
Depending on temperature, cloud cover, and air velocity factors, efficiency is from sixty five to eighty four percent efficient. Yes.

In order to clarify the term "efficiency," the total amount of sunlight falling on the collector in terms of energy....
Can be retained directly at the percentage of sunlight contact.

The average solar cell right now can get a little over ten percent from on the shelf commercial technology.
Correct.

That represents a seven fold increase. That would do it!
There is also another contribution which is also highly effective. It is a combination solar and wind collector.

Why is it so effective?
One form of natural energy propels the other so that no outside energy is required to start the motion or keep the process functioning.

That is more of a systems combination than a component improvement.
Yes, but it is a very shardy whirly gig. Remember: "That which includes is Positive."

Tao Song.

THE JUMP TO MIND MECHANICS

We would like to talk about the "Jump" and try to understand that process. Can you tell us more about the "Jump?"
At this Now, the objective for this Mother is to accomplish The Jump to Mind Mechanics. This is a Rate increase in which forgotten mental and psychic abilities will be re-remembered. All humans will relearn telathing, teleportation, and mind augmentation with crystals through which many different kinds of work can be accomplished; even the potential of direct matter manipulation with thought.

To achieve The Jump completely, a rate increase, a dimension transcendence to a higher Rate of function is required. The initial stage of The Jump to Mind Mechanics is being experienced even at this Now. The possibilities are becoming greater that this Jump can be accomplished. There are a continually increasing number of people becoming aware of the power of thought energy; an increasing belief in the potential of Mind Mechanics. The Rate Jump is being considered seriously; the build-up to the Rate increase, which we call The Jump.

What triggers The Jump?
The Jump is accomplished through the working Balance between planet, technology, and spirituality. It is the culmination of the desire to augment these three aspects simultaneously for the greater creative potential. When The Jump is accomplished, there will be much greater leeway to create different concepts, different technologies, different ways of being. A kind of graduated creativity will occur. If one was considering art school, The Jump would be graduation from stick-figure crayon drawing to oil paints. Once the basic preparatory knowledge has been accomplished, The Jump to Mind Mechanics, and Rate increase, and the creativity towards Positive and Balance will be enhanced.

That example is revealing in terms of growth, in terms of expansion. What happens to an individual experiencing The Jump?
There are many physical changes. There are sensation changes for the body. All body senses become more enhanced, varied, and perceptive. There is conscious access to knowing and remembering of knowledge acquired throughout previous lives. For the individual, The Jump will bring spherical perspective as opposed to linear. There is the ability to move from place to place with thought; to "think" there and

"be" there, whether it is individual travel or an object a person wishes to send or send for. It can be "thought" there when The Jump Rate is accomplished.

That is what you referred to as teleportation?
    Correct.

What about communications between individuals?
    These can be either telathed or spoken. There will need to be telathing instruction and much practice in order to strengthen individual mind shields so that everyone does not hear everyone speaking at once.

Are there other abilities besides telathing and teleporting. These two abilities will seem beyond belief. Are there others?
    There are infinite kinds of new technologies and augmentations which can be relearned.

I do not understand that. Can you explain that?
    It is use of various forms of matter manipulation through thought. After the Rate increase, if a physician treated a body which was malfunctioning or injured, the physicians thought energies, enhanced through crystals using light-sound, could manipulate the tissues to accomplish healing without any invasive procedure required. A physician could "Think" a heart valve corrected; "Think" a malignant brain growth neutralized and removed. Gene defects or hereditary diseases could be resolved with thought enhanced by crystals.

Would you review the conversation we just had that was not recorded[46]?
    In one exchange, we were all discussing the potentials of achieving The Rate Jump individual to individual, whether it is a cumulative Jump or whether some individuals achieve The Jump Rate first and then a more gradual collective process ensues. We stated, Yes, it is a gradual process. We stated it is a snowball effect.
    The question was asked: "If a person wishes to achieve The Rate Jump, is it possible to accomplish it through meditation? Can the individual's guides or backers assist in this?" We were stating that this

---

[46]About twenty minutes of a very interesting conversation was not recorded.

method is, of course, possible.

We were also discussing the complexities of communication between dimensions. If a person accelerated into The Jump Rate/Dimension, would it be as difficult to establish communications with Non-Physical Plane beings as it is at the present Third Dimension Rate? Would there be a discrepancy in communication with those who have accomplished The Jump and those who have not. We stated that there would necessarily be great assistance given to persons who were literally carried through to the new Rate by more expanded and prepared persons. Therefore, it is of greater assistance to maintain an "inclusive" vein of thought rather than "exclusive".

There was a discussion in regards to the question of whether or not other individuals, over the eons, have achieved The Jump Rate and whether they continued to function physically in this dimension. We spoke of various Lamas and Buddhist recluses who have achieved The Jump Rate through self deprivation and isolation, but we stated that that method is a kind of "backing into Enlightenment." If, in order to achieve Jump Rate, the concentration, attention, and awareness focus is accomplished by "excluding" all things; by divorcing the individual from The Whole; by segregating from the dimension, then the achievement is not a contributing Positive action. Thought, action and unity are required to accomplish The Jump Rate. Benefits only to the individual do not make a Positive contribution to The Whole of The Whole including all other humans. Individual Jump accomplishments, therefore, are actions which produce only stasis. It is not Negative, but it is not Active Positive. It is simply maintenance of the status quo. The most Positive approach to accomplishing The Jump is, of course, to include "all things" for the benefit of "all things."

It is not necessary to "exclude" or seperate in order to focus sufficient thought awareness or attention to accomplish The Jump. The including: the practice of "allowing" the stimuli awareness - in terms of thought and action, is how to positively accomplish The Jump Rate. Then as the snow ball picks up momentum rolling down the hill and reaches a critical mass point, all other humans are transcended to the Mind Mechanics rate of function, they Jump together as a whole.

This is a somewhat compressed version of our previous conversation. Did you wish to ask questions for elaboration?

On the snowball effect, certain individuals will make The Jump ahead of others. As their numbers accumulate, we will reach some sort of critical state. Is that correct?

Correct.

And then in a instant, literally a second, the entire population .....?
And the planet Rate also.

And the planet will make the leap?
Correct.

What percentage is that critical mass state?
You had previously stated 3 percent of total world population. Three percent of the population is sufficient.

The remaining 97 percent of the population is going to be very surprised at their new abilities.
Correct. And those who were prepared will be spending much time counseling others and assisting those in shock because of not being prepared. Yes.

You mentioned Followers of the Law of One earlier. Are they going to be The Jump precipitators?
The Followers of The Law of One are all ready starting that small snowball rolling. Their increased awareness understands that humans and the planet cannot exist independently. In order for each to survive the other must survive. The awareness of that factor, that this entire planet is your Home, your Mother, your place of Being, is the understanding that is precipitating the momentum for The Jump. This is where we were discussing the linear years of time to achieve The Jump provided there is a choice to make The Jump.

If we decide not to have a polar shift, and we actuate that, what would be the projection of our decision with regards to the time until The Jump? In other words, we are trying to do a kind of, "If we decide this, and if we decide that,"... then how many years to The Jump?
Taking those projected "ifs" into consideration, seventy-five to one hundred years could see the accomplishment of the Rate Dimension Jump to Mind Mechanics. Seventy-five to one hundred years, yes.

There was another question about the last three years?
If the thought patterns - the mode of thinking, the actions, the attitude, and the intent of human beings - had remained the same as they

were three years previous to Now, all would have possibly, stretching the linear time function, twenty to thirty years before the Mother shiself would undertake a rebalancing action. The Mother would ensure shis own survival and Balance with a polar shift.

In the intervening time, in the last three years, however, have we altered our intention?
People have accomplished a vast awakening. The tie between the Planet and shis living beings and living systems has been realized. The actions which have followed this realization are coming closer and closer to Beneficial Wholism Assessment. You have done very well in terms of extending the reprieve for yourselves and your planet through "Consideration." You have accomplished an extension of five years for one; over the last three, nearly five years. Of course the intent has become more focused in the last three years. That is a considerable reprieve in terms of Planet/People coordination and intent[47].

Excellent. Let's see if we can recall some of the other areas. Have we missed any?
There is one area we wish to discuss. The question concerning how the individual achieves The Jump Rate increase. It is possible to accomplish The Jump in as little as five minutes. The Rate Jump is similar to enlightenment. It is the focus of awareness and coordination of thought and action. Using a large quantity of rhetoric we asked previously, "How many people pay acute attention to what they do?" Not only what they do, but what they think about while they are doing. It is the focus of **attention** that makes The Jump possible for an individual. It can happen while a person is washing dishes; when a person becomes "one" with the action they are undertaking - **Being what you do.**
We also offered a practice exercise. Practice: "Being green." Practice being your action. Ask, as you perform an action, "What does it feel like? What does it look like? How does it feel as I do it? What do I smell? What do I hear?" It is including all incoming thoughts and coordinating them with the action that makes The Jump possible. It is "being what you do" completely - in the Now moment. It is the desire to practice and accomplish this as you function within the whole of

---

[47]The projected polar shift date has been pushed back 3x5 = 15 years in the last three years.

humanity that carries all forward to the critical mass   and The Rate Jump.

So going up into a cave and isolating yourself from the world and meditating and reducing the amount of stimulus will...
   Will achieve an individual Jump Rate, but it is static. It is not a detriment, but it is not a contribution, for it does not augment the intent of The Whole of the Whole.

Just paying attention? Just focusing?
   It is necessary to remember that focus is "including." It is allowing the entirety of the moment as opposed to excluding parts. If you are busy attempting to push away thoughts instead of embracing all thoughts of the moment, then you have triggered The Law of Resistance. You only push away what you are attempting most to achieve. It is the "whole" of a thing, including the thoughts, which contributes more rapidly to the state of consciousness which precipitates The Jump.

Instead of concentrating on one idea or object, concentrate on what my hands are feeling, what my eyes see, what my nose smells,.....
   Exactly.

Forget the sequence and.....
   Be.

And do not come out of that moment, that instantaneous presence?
   Yes, because of that, you can observe all moments sequentially and be all moments simultaneously. This may seem esoteric, but in actuality it is totally practical. The Jump is accomplished in the moment - melding time and function simultaneously. The factor of "time" opens up another discussion.

Time, yes. When you make The Jump, do you remember all your history, your past lives?
   Correct. You will be able to recall what you have learned and experienced through many lifetimes.

Does that mean, for example, if, in a previous lifetime, I was a carpenter in 1910, I would have that set of memories?
   You have those memories already. After The Rate Jump, people will have the ability to access the experiences on a conscious level.

With such abilities, much of our technology and things we think are necessary, are not going to be needed.

It is quite possible.

I was thinking about our transportation and communication systems.

There would be the possibility to think yourself to a place. Correct.

Teleporting?

Correct.

Would that also apply to material things?   Could I teleport five pounds of flour down the street?

With certain tools for thought augmentation, of course.

And perhaps special training.

Crystal augmenters would be needed; but with practice this is feasible.

Telephones will be to some extent obsolete.

It is essential that personal shield courtesy be relearncd so that everyone does not hear everyone all the time. That would be quite a jumble. Establishment of a mind shield prior to telathing is essential. This telathing courtesy is similar to a phone number or a call sign. Each individual has shis specific call. Then speaking mind to mind can be accomplished in comfort. It can be jolting or irritating when a person speaks mentally without first "knocking."

Can you give us some exercises for people who want to develop their Mind Mechanics? There are several different areas. Joy, telepathy, remembering past lives, using crystal enhancers, matter manipulations, and any others that you feel you should be discussed.

The basic rule or thought to embrace before starting on any Mind Mechanic exercise is: Pay Attention! Thinking about what you think, observing minutia, learning to be aware of detail. Focus is not so much clearing the mind, as it is paying attention to the thoughts that occur in the instant that they occur. "Schooling your thoughts" is an old cliche, but that is what "paying attention" means. Do not energize thoughts you do not want. If you are paying attention to your thoughts and one enters that you do not like, acknowledge the thought. Do not try to push the thought out. Immediately acknowledge it. Consciously replace it with one of Positive intent, one that encompasses your ideal. Do not allow Negative thoughts to play hide and seek with you. Acknowledge them and dismiss them. Then purposefully think or state out loud your ideal replacement for that Negative thought. This may not seem like an exercise in Mind Mechanics at all, but it is the basic one.

In many systems of physical skill, the foundation is the most important thing.

People can learn to pay attention to what they think and to train their thoughts and mental focus by speaking thoughts out loud. Speaking aloud is the way to develop mastery of **Light-Sound Energy**. The combination of Light and Sound is the energy that thought is made of. Employing both kinds of energy and observing how those energies feel when they are used accomplishes **focus**. If you speak aloud, you are using Sound energy. That Sound-Rate energy in combination with Light is contained in thought and focuses the intent. Note the feeling which occurs within your brain. Learning to observe how this feels will give you the ability to consciously recall that feeling and, with that memory, trigger the area which can send a thought, receive a thought, or enhance a thought with augmenters. All desire to create and experience joy. Correct?

Sure.

Six or seven times each day state the word "Joy" aloud. It will make you smile automatically. Then for fifteen seconds think of those things which bring you joy: Green trees, blue sky, the smell of new cut grass, a baby's giggle, a nice hot bath, a lollipop. The investment of focused thought energy creates seven to the seventh power in Positive energy augmentation of that which was initially invested. If you spend fifteen seconds thinking of joy, your Positive thought investment is magnified seven to the seventh power times. If you do that exercise three times a day using thoughts of healing, love, Balance, joy , you are creating great potential for those ideas to become reality.

Now if you wish to practice telepathy, a partner is helpful. Set a time of day, perhaps when each goes on an errand. Agree that one will be a sender the other will be a receiver. At some time during the errand, the sender will send a thought: a color or a fruit. The receiver will attempt to discern what is sent. Each should write down what was sent and what was received before re-uniting. The more this is practiced the more effective and successful telepathy will become. Make it a game not work. You can start with one word or one object. It is easy to see how to build from there. Crystals are another factor to consider. This can be of great assistance.

How is that?
It is necessary for us to give only very general information regarding Mind Mechanics enhancers at this Now. We have spoken of previous civilization and how crystals were used greatly in connection with Mind Mechanics. The Mind Mechanics were developed extensively first before enhancing tools, to any complex degree, were attempted. Most previous technological civilizations used faceted crystals and gems. This is quite intricate and risky if full command of Mind Mechanics is not achieved first. Do you see?
We need to develop our natural abilities before we apply the enhancers?
Correct. At least to a greater degree than exists at this Now. Using these enhancers to harness Thought/Light/Sound for lasing, teleportation, or surgery requires a highly developed refinement of Mind Mechanics and enhancer coordination.

That is pretty far down the road in terms of our development.
Correct. With a smiley poke, we would say, "Start practicing."

In terms of the general development of Mind Mechanics, we have laid down the foundations. It seems that developing these abilities could take a little bit of time. Perhaps generations.
Not necessarily. It depends on how serious the understanding that these are inherent skills and only need be practiced regularly to reawaken them from dormancy. The assumption that these are skills which can be relearned is a step towards recovering them.

Like learning to read. If there are people around that can use and demonstrate telepathy, it becomes teachable so to speak.
We have outlined a method of lessons which you can begin any time you wish.

Is there anything else you wish to say about Mind Mechanics practice?
Yes. Practice.

That sounds like master Kuo[48] talking about Tai Chi.

Exactly. For telathing: You will find through practice which person is a better sender and which is a better receiver. Each can assist the other to acquire the right sensation, to identify the correct feeling in the brain for sending or receiving. Then each can teach the other shis skill. Practice in Joy, have fun.

Tao Song.

---

[48]Kuo Lin Ying, 1895-1983

PREVIOUS CIVILIZATIONS AND POLAR SHIFTS

According to what you have stated there have been polar shifts in the past. Could you elaborate on why these happened ?
All of the previous Circles[49] of highly advanced civilizations have succumbed to polar shifts. When the intent of humans and the direction of their technology becomes solely self-aggrandizing and in conflict with the Balance of the Mother planet, then there is a polar axis shift in order to ensure continuation of the Mother's life. Many of the behaviors of humans today are similar to those which have thrown other civilizations into Negative imbalance and polar shift. There is much "slow" or Negative energy being created in this Now.

Individuals have the power to create energy with their thoughts. If Negative thought is backed by Negative action the planetary eco-system - shis very life - is in jeopardy. When this occurs the Mother will resort to shis own self-defense mechanisms in order to neutralize the Negative energy.

What we are about to say may seem confusing, possibly too metaphysical. However, it is a truth. There is a connection between the Physical and the Metaphysical. The Planet shiself has a rate of consciousness. Shis is a **living being**. Within the Galactic eco-system and Universal eco-system this planet is essential. Shis part in that Balance must continue. Therefore the Mother will neutralize Negative energies created by humans so that Balance of the Physical Plane eco-system is sustained.

Yes, there have been many polar shifts. The last major polar shift was approximately 7500 years ago. This shift displaced the continent you call Atlantis from the region near the equator to where it is now located - Antarctica. Because of this shift, the entire global population was reduced to very few in number. Only two percent of the population existing at that time survived the shift and many more perished in the storms and cataclysms which occurred afterwards.

Before this last shift, there was a long period of time when ecological and planetary Balance was stable. The North Pole, previous to the last shift, was situated in Lake Chad, Africa. The topography

---

[49]Circle of a civilization - A civilization's rise, development, and subsequent demise due to a polar shift.

surrounding Lake Chad evidences an immense depression. Also, Lake Chad is a land locked lake with no feeders and no sea outlet.

It is possible to chart the areas where previous North poles have been located. There is one in Hudson Bay area. Another North Pole has been the greater Amazon basin area. When poles are located over water there is potential for a much longer period without a shift occurring. When located on land area, this time frame is shortened.

Was there a long period before the last shift and the one previous to the last shift?

Yes, It was a long interval. That civilization maintained Balance for a considerable period. This was the Athlenta civilization. You call it Atlantis. It survived for nearly fifty thousand years before the Balance of technology, thought, and action moved out of the Positive and a shift occurred. Before the Athlenta civilization was the Muyon civilization. It is not the same one you know as Lemuria. The Lemuran civilization preceded the Muyon.

How many times have civilizations risen on the planet and caused environmental damage which resulted in the Mother engaging shis self defense mechanisms and shift of the poles?

We wish to offer this again, as of a kind of explanation. The Design for human interaction with the Mother in Physical Plane is: **Spiritual and Technological Equilibrium**; technology becoming directly reflective of spirituality. This is the blueprint plan for Balance on this Mother planet. Therefore, when these two factors develop in conflict with each other, the entire living system of the Mother begins to build Negative energy. If this Negative energy becomes too extensive to neutralize by humans, the Mother shiself will use shis own method: a shift of the poles.

There have been nine previous technological civilizations on this planet.

Could you outline previous technical civilizations, commenting on approximate dates, cause of their end, level of achievement, and other   significant factors to help us understand their situation?

We would wish to state that the most useful - we will not use the term significant - the most familiar examples of prior technological civilizations can be outlined by using three or four examples as opposed to making a complete linear list.

The Quoli Trior Sa civilization is the earliest. This civilization was in its height seven hundred fifty thousand years ago. There was complete use of Mind Mechanics and enhancers for those Mind Mechanics. The use of Mind Mechanics does not mean they had achieved the Jump. Many had dubious intent even though they knew how to use Mind Mechanics. Solar energy was the main source of power in that Now. Most of the prolonged, successful, high technology Circles used varied forms of solar power. In the Quoli Trior Sa Circle there was communication and interaction with "People" of other planets, other Mothers. The Quoli Trior Sa did not travel to other planets. However, there were extensive extraterrestrial visits to the Quoli Trior Sa. One of the reasons, the main reason the Quoli Trior Sa Circle was obliterated or ruined was due to a group with mal-intent who sent for energy augmenters. These were Mind Mechanic augmentation tools; much more powerful than crystals. These augmenters were from another planet and were highly advanced. These thought augmenters are called Krom Kromu. That is the plural.   A single tool would be called a Krom. Within a period of twenty five years that civilization was totally destroyed. The civilization was obliterated through the Krom wars. Humans used the Krom Kromu to war upon each other. That is why there is not the smallest evidence of this civilization; not any structure or artifact. The Krom Kromu could accomplish total disintegration of matter through thought augmentation. When used for Negative, they are a frighteningly powerful tool. After the Krom wars, there were very few of the Followers of the Law of One remaining. They retreated into obscurity, hiding to avoid the Krom wars. They searched for and gathered the Krom Kromu together and had these tools returned.

The Quoli Trior Sa Circle, until its final demise, was one of the most successful and Balanced civilizations. During its height it had a global government and a common culture which maintained Balance for nearly two hundred thousand years.

Two polar shifts within one hundred years occurred in order to neutralize the accumulated energy imbalance and Negativity produce by the Krom wars. There is still a small area of land at this Now which is totally sterile as a result of the Krom wars. Even at this Now, the smallest bacteria or fungi when introduced into the soil cannot survive. It is near the Nazca plain in Peru.

What causes that?

It was caused because the Krom Kromu could emit a sterilizing field beam. The residual effect is similar to half life of nuclear waste. It takes time to neutralize. There is a residual that has remained. It is not harmful to touch this soil, but nothing can grow in it. It will not interact with an ecological food chain. That area will not enter the link, the system link.

How much area is involved?
It is a relatively small area, possibly a little more than one acre.

That provides opportunity for scientific verification if we could pin-point that location.
It is necessary to copter to the sight. The designs and markings are considered a world wonder by that country and are protected. In truth, these markings are landing strips and runways for ancient aircraft and space craft.

Now to continue. The time and effort required for humanity to recover from those two pivots was considerable. The next civilization, The Lletrurid, was much more spiritually advanced than technologically advanced. The next advanced technological civilization was the Lemuran Circle some five hundred thousand years after the Quoli Trior Sa. This civilization also developed a common culture and a global government. Solar energy was the power source for the technology. There was an intense focus on physics and astronomy. They developed, as we will define, a usable anti-gravity force. This force was not successfully managed. The process used to contain the force, so the force could be used, was not regulated. Its manufacture caused a type of Negative radiation. Ignorance and negligence is what caused the deterioration of the Lemuran culture. It was not done intentionally through the desire of the people to create Negative. It occurred because the effects of constant use of the anti-gravity material were not discovered and assessed accurately until the imbalance became so widespread and extensive that retrieval of Balance was impossible. The Lemuran culture existed for seventy five thousand years before the Negative energy build up caused its destruction. Two hundred forty thousand years ago the Lemuran culture was at its Golden Age. A complete devastation of that culture did not occur. There was a major cataclysm but the knowledge and efficiency of survival technology was such that all was not demolished because of the polar shift. The recovery of the new civilization, the Muyon, was quite rapid. The details of anti gravity force were recorded, but it was decided that this energy source was not viable and would not be used. At that time the most effective energy alternative was cut and "keyed"[50] crystals. The high priesthood or scholars were trained to integrate their mind patterns to the patterns of the cut crystals, thus "keying" with them. The Major Force crystals were diamonds. Their power could be used to enhance many aspects of solar energy when used in conjunction with thought. The crystals could be used to combine light with sound; for lasers, for lifters. This culture has left much evidence in terms of buildings or structures. Remnants of these are still present at this time. The Muyon culture developed the concept and construction of pyramids; also the techniques of building in stone without binders - without substances to stick the stones together. The stones are fit so impeccably because they were lased to fit. If a corner was too large, it could be whisked off with a laser on the site.

It is impressive to use lasers for cutting large blocks of stone. That requires tremendous power focus.

This is accomplished in conjunction with thought energy. As with the many previous civilizations, Mind Mechanics were highly developed.

At the end of the Muyon civilization, there was a global war with extensive use of biological chemicals. The war was a sudden occurrence. There were so few people left of the Muyon civilization that the residue, the physical carnage overloaded the Mother's processes. The chemicals affected all species of animal life. There is scientific and geologic collaboration even at this Now where entire species extinction is recorded in the geologic time table. The Muyon civilization ended about sixty thousand years ago.

Were the remaining people affected genetically by that bio chemical war?

Susceptibility to virus occurred. Previous to this, the House, the body, had much better resistance to virus.

A bio-chemical war followed by a polar shift is very devastating. How many people survived that?

Two hundred fifty Followers of the Law of One in two different

---

[50]Keyed - mind linked with the Positive intent of a specific person. No one could use a keyed crystal except the person to whom the crystal was mind - linked.

facilities below ground and fifty in a shielded suspension field. Only two percent of the surface populace survived. Global population was reduced to less than a million persons.

The Muyon civilization is followed by the Athlenta, that which you call Atlantis. The Athlenta civilization developed rapidly because the remaining Followers of the Law of One had access to the extensive Repository[51] information.

Now it is important to understand that each of the last three major cultures height is less sophisticated than the one which preceded it. Some technology and abilities are continually degenerating over that sequence of three civilizations.

The Athlenta Circle began with a great disadvantage. After the polar shift and the loss of the Muyon civilization, the old research and manufacture of the anti-gravity stones was re-instituted. The Athlenta redeveloped the Lemuran anti-gravity force. A specific material which we call "stones" was imbued with this power of anti-gravity. As the stones degenerated, intense radiation was released. During the later period of the Athlenta civilization, the stones were arranged in specific patterns in various locations producing radioactive barriers or fences. These barriers were used to ensure control of the general population through the fear of mortal injury. The use of this energy was so extensive that the people operating the neutralizing crystals could not handle the overload of radiation produced by the stones. Many crystals were destroyed in the attempt.

So they lost control of their technology rather suddenly. These anti-gravity stones seem to have been a problem for three different civilizations. Is this one of those humps that every technical civilization has to get over? Speaking of anti-gravity will generate interest among the scientific community and they will desire to develop, or employ, it once again.

Previous civilizations developed a process in which the capability to initiate anti-gravity was confined in material compounds, "stones," which could release or create anti-gravity for the purpose of

---

[51]Repository - There are three main repositories. One is located in the Andes, one in Tibet, and another in Egypt. These are combination warehouse-libraries. Each highly advanced civilization has used these to store their history, scientific, and medical technology and a variety of machines representative of the civilizations technological advancement.

transport. Many transportation vehicles, land and air, had drives which used anti-gravity stones. The process used to imbue the "stones" with the anti-gravity capability is what caused the Negative, radioactive by product. We wish to state here, that all processes that divide, whether they be at the atomic level, a method of energy production, or human interaction, produce cumulative Negative energy. That is why fission is a dirty energy process. It is energy based on a process which "divides" rather than "includes." Fusion, because it is a process which combines, can be a Positive energy production process. Radioactive, or any waste, for that matter, is difficult to deal with.

Is it that they were ignorant? Is it possible to produce these anti-gravity 'stones' without having harmful waste resulting?
When there is desire to acquire, use, and accrue more than is necessary for harmony and Balance, the detrimental aspects of a process are intentionally overlooked. When this occurs, for the purpose of self aggrandizement, or affluence, creation of Negative energy occurs.

It sounds like greed.
You are quite correct. Self aggrandizement creates division and thereby Negativity.

So, there is nothing inherently wrong with anti-gravity except that the most expedient way to production is dirty and the clean up effort could be easily overlooked by those focusing on immediate proceeds. Sounds familiar.
Exactly. However there are clean sources and methods of energy available. When people want to avoid the discomfort of the interim conversion from dirty sources to clean sources, the more familiar, but dirty processes, are kept in use.

It is important to get the dates of the various civilizations clear. Can you go over that again?
We find it quite gigglely that dates hold such importance. We see that it is more important to understand that once the height of that civilization was reached, it maintained its Golden Age until the last one hundred years before the rapid decline and ensuing pole shift occurred.
The Athlenta civilization lasted for fifty thousand years. The pivot which preceded this occurred fifty five hundred years previous to that. It is helpful to understand that we count the beginning of the civilization from the point that civilization reaches its height. This

should give you the key.

So it took the Athlenta 5500 years to rise up again after the pivot which ended the Muyon civilization.
Then the Muyon from its height lasted seventy five thousand years. The recovery period from the Lemuran demise was much quicker so it was only some three thousand years to recover from the Lemuran polar shift.
However the Lemuran culture lasted nearly one hundred thousand years. Previous to that was the Lletrurid culture. The Lletrurid civilization, in comparison to the others, is a very short Circle and not as technically advanced. The Lletrurid were very spiritually advanced and Positive, but the Balance between consciousness and technology was not equal. The dates here become very malleable and tend to blend together for the Lemuran was beginning it's rise at the same time the Lletrurid was declining. Although there was a polar shift, it was prepared for. Therefore most of the technology and knowledge was preserved. The greatest time gap is taken up in the attempt to recover from the Krom wars after the demise of the Quoli Trior Sa civilization. There were nearly five hundred thousand years between the demise of the Quoli Trior Sa Circle and the relatively small Lletrurid civilization.

What kind of technology or what kind of research can reveal the location of former poles? How does one go about examining the history of the earth or the geology in these areas to define the location of a pole?
Using mathematics, there is a way of calculating the weight/pressure which build up on the poles to the point where, at the rate of spin that the earth has, this weight cannot be supported at that rate of spin. As the ice mass and weight builds up at the polar caps, the Earth develops an orbital wobble. Eventually the mass will reach a critical point and the North Pole will tilt some 83 degrees towards the equator where the weight distribution is more in equilibrium with the forces produced by the Earth's spin. If the location of the previous pole is known, calculations in reverse can locate the other previous pole locations.
The physical action of a shift is not based solely on the progression of the physical phenomena from a polar ice build up. It is also dependant upon the thought energy and action created and

Summary of Previous Technical Civilizations
Counting Backward from the Present

Description of period	Approximate length of Period in years	Remarks
Athlenta pivot recovery	7,500	Still underway
Golden age of Athlenta	50,000	
Muyon pivot recovery	5,500	
Golden age of Muyon	75,000	
Lemuran pivot recovery	3,000	
Golden age of Lemuran	75,000	
Lletrurid pivot recovery	500	
Golden age of Lletrurid	5,000	Technology not highly developed
Quoli Trior Sa pivots recovery	500,000	Severe damage from Krom wars
Golden age of Quoli Trior Sa	200,000	

---

expressed by humans. It is connected to the Balance between Spirituality and Technology.

Is there any way to make physical measurements to determine the locations of the poles; for verification purposes? Would doing a core sample and examination of the direction of the magnetic fields, or assessing the geologic structure of various layers in the area give definite evidence there was a rotating body?

Both core samples and magnetic tests of geologic layers could be used to read previous pole locations.

There are also structures left from the Lemuran civilization that are here to day. The statues in Easter Island, the foundation and two cap stones of The Giant's Dance - Stonehenge.   There are four foundation structures and two complete walls in Machupichu, Peru which remain as evidence.   There is also, the little known, plas-steel floor in the great Lamasery in Tibet. This has a Mosaic cover, but it is there.

What happened to what should be a rather massive archeological record?   For example, skeletons, tools, buildings, machinery, particularly plas-steel which should not deteriorate.   I can understand the damage from sub-sonic winds, mile high tidal waves and so on, but if two percent of the people survived, there should be a lot of relics.

Correct. These have been saved. Repositories located in three different areas have a carefully selected preserve of records, technology and various mechanicals[52]. There are also many areas which still show above ground. But scientists deny that these are what they are. The fitted stones in Machupichu are close to 300,000 years old. The temple remnants of the great king Ata Ualpa are from the Muyon Circle. These stones are fit with such precision; sized and matched stones of smooth basalt, completely foreign to the area. The geologists and archaeologists deny the evidence which is in front of their faces. Now there are a great many artifacts which simply cannot be reached. They are under water. However, those which are available are denied. There are many relics packed in boxes in the store rooms of the Smithsonian Institute. There are even mechanicals which are in glass show cases, misnamed, misunderstood, and assumed to be much younger than they are. The Hope[53] diamond, the blue diamond, is a re-cut of what is left of a much larger barrel shaped "song crystal" which is over 12,000 years old. It is thought to be cursed, because it has been cleaved out of the shape it was cut and keyed for, and the energies are discordant.

It will be difficult to convince people who are knowledgeable in the field.   They will not believe that 7,500 years ago there was a civilization in Peru which had high technology, yet not have obvious remnants.   What happened to the skeletons of the people, burial grounds and things like that?

There have been many of these skeletons, burial grounds, etc., discovered.

And ignored?

Exactly.   Remember, in this area of which you speak, the religious system, the political and economic system do not offer open-

---

[52] Mechanicals - Machines or technological tools.

[53]The Hope diamond is on display in the Smithsonian Institute.

minded assistance or tolerance. Those scientists who could verify the remaining evidence are not allowed to examine or explore the artifacts.

Tao Song.

POLAR SHIFT MECHANICS

We want to discuss polar shift mechanics. Is it beneficial to provide our scientists with enough details on polar shift mechanics so that this can be included in our current version of geophysics and history?

Not many scientists, as a consortium, or a group, put much stock in this concept, reality. It is beneficial, however, to make these facts available. What specifics do you wish regarding the mechanics of a polar shift.

How long does a shift take?

This can vary depending upon the mass weight of ice at each pole. If you wish a norm, or average, this 82 to 84 degree shift from polar axis to equator takes three hours. Which, of course, in terms of distance and size of this Mother is rapid.

We are dealing with norms. What we could do to solve that problem is use the last shift for reference.

There is not a significant difference. The most recent polar shift was 2 hours 40 to 45 minutes. This is near the norm. The most recent shift was slightly more rapid because both poles were located over land masses.

What were the peak velocities achieved during that shift?

The peak velocities were close to 2,700 miles per hour on the surface relative to the previous pole position.

Where did the previous North Pole arrive at after the shift?

The previous North Pole became Lake Chad, Africa. This land locked lake is the last remnant of the previous North Pole.

It appears that there has been some continental drift if that was an eighty three degree shift. The current location of Lake Chad is closer to seventy eight degrees now.

The settling of the Mother's outer skin can cause discrepancies in terms of degrees[54]. It takes seven to ten years for the cataclysm precipitated by a polar shift to settle into relative tranquility. Therefore, you are correct. There are differences in the location after a period of time.

DIAGRAM OF THREE PREVIOUS POLAR SHIFTS

---

[54]There are also well understood dynamic effects, such as the nutation of a top, that could result in a partial return in a system which has less than critical damping.

The approximate locations of previous north poles and the path of the poles during shifts are shown in the diagram. The locations are determined from the given locations, Lake Chad, the Hudson Bay, and the Amazon Basin. These locations correspond with shifts of about 78, 80, and 70 degrees. In the diagram the arrow represents a shift with the previous pole at the head and the new pole at the tail. The paths of the pole locations can be readily seen with the following procedure. Place a globe so that the Amazon Basin of South America is at the top. Rotate the globe so that the Hudson Bay is at the top. This rotation was the shift at the end of the Lemuran civilization. Rotating the globe until Lake Chad in Africa is at the top is the Muyon shift. Rotating the globe until the present North Pole is at the top is the Athlenta shift.

Since the North Pole has shifted a certain amount, has the previous South Pole shifted in the same direction; exactly opposite from the previous North Pole?

Yes.

In general, what type of forces are involved?   Is it strictly gravitational and classical mechanics as we know it?

This area of discussion may cause many scientists to get "cold feet," be skeptical[55]. However, it is in accordance with Physical Law. The impetus of a polar shift is also connected to what you call the Metaphysical Energies. There is no technology in your society today to measure Metaphysical Energy.   A pivot, also, depends upon the

---

[55]The concept of a pole shift has been put forward by several individuals in recent times, including Hugh Auchincloss Brown and Charles Hapgood. The forward to Hapgood's 1958 *Earth's Shifting Crust* is written by Albert Einstein.   The non-response of the scientific community, as a whole, to Hapgood's work is described by John White in *Pole Shift*, which is an excellent compilation of information regarding pole shifts from a variety of sources. According to White, Einstein's strongest doubts were regarding the ice cap mechanism proposed to account for the displacement of the Earth's outer shell. Hapgood made extensive revisions in this regard a dozen years later in *The Path of the Pole*. Brown's *Cataclysms of the Earth*, gives an account of polar shifts which are similar to the Fairns' description, 80 degree tilts occurring in a single day. He also identifies the same two previous pole locations, Lake Chad and the Hudson Bay.

cumulative "Aura Energy" of the planet shiself. This is directly related to the thought energies and creations which ensouled species - humans - generate themselves. The deciding factor is the energy output of ensouled sapient beings.

That includes the whales, dolphins, and porpoises as well as ourselves.
On this Mother, yes.

Perhaps a quantitative approach would be more revealing to geophysicists. Could a computer model simulate the shift dynamics to within two percent accuracy?
We would wish to offer you this for thought. The project is possible. But what you are offering with this information is even greater. You will spark others to initiate that of which you speak. If you offer these hypotheses, there will be persons interested in setting this dynamic model on a computer as a creative project of their own.

It may be helpful to delineate the general guidelines that would establish the model, to give some hints. We could use a model - equations, which would consist of spherical shells matched to the materials' properties of different layers within the earth.
And you feel that this working model outlined or assisted with certain equations would be what you are wanting to offer.

Yes, and to define the model physically, or conceptually so that it is easy to apply the equations. A simple approach is to use a two-component model, a shell and sphere. The sphere is connected to the outer shell with a fluid interface. The two are rotating, assumably, about the same axis.
Correct.

Then, we introduce into the symmetrical system some lumped masses which are sightly off center of the polar positions.
We send you are large smile. Proceed.

Then we can use the equations of rigid body dynamics - differential equations which describe the system. A computer can solve the equations and simulate the motion for a set of initial conditions - assuming the lumped masses are fixed to the surface of the spherical shell, and defining the characteristic constants for the

terms which connect the interior sphere to the exterior shell. For the fluid coupling this would be drag coefficients and friction coefficients. With that information and rigid body dynamics, it should be very easy to compute the future evolution of the system. We could vary the masses and so on to see what would happen.

This is correct. This is theoretically accurate. One factor to be constantly aware of is that you are the technologically advancing ensouled species which is becoming more intelligent and more aware of exactly how those dynamics work. Therefore, the whole process can be prevented if the essential Balance between humans and the planet's workings itself are recognized, as you say, in time.

It is the recognition that humans must be in the Balanced system as an integral unit that gives them the recognition of this as a potentially systematic occurrence on this specific Mother. Humans can avoid the need to calculate the dynamics of polar shifts through their own attempts at coordinating their technology with that Balanced system of the mother. Therefore, those masses which build up in the form of ice on each polar cap can be advantageously and constructively reduced by humans in their desire to maintain their technology, their civilization and their Balance with the ecology of the planet. This may not seem logical, but that is what humans are working towards, to make that dimension Jump.

Aligning the Z axis of the coordinate system along the axis of rotation of the globe provides a reference frame to define the moments of inertia that characterize the crust.

Correct. You must also remember that because there is fluid between the core and crust there will be some flow drag. There will also be a flux or rippling of the outer crust layers and on settling, this can create a backwash. That is what causes the discrepancy in degrees of axis pivot from pole to equator and later, the offset.

Before we get too far into this general model, let's run some ball park numbers.....

We have assessed those mass and weight extensions you have. Most are within workable allowable measures. There is one factor which you have overlooked. It is the yaw.

The yaw. That would relate to the asymmetries in the rotational inertias.

Correct, and the location of the weight mass of the present

poles.

A coordinate system with an axis through the center of the polar ice weight masses can be used and also one with the axis through the center of rotation.
One is much more stable in rotation about the axis.

What is the angle between those two axes?
From the perpendicular it is four degrees angle of yaw. A wobble of four degrees.

Does the rotational angular velocity of the earth - before and after a shift - change as viewed by an observer in space traveling along the solar orbit with the earth?
Picture a spinning top. It has a Balanced rotation of spin. If drops of wax are added at the top axis of rotation, the increasing weight will cause a yaw wobble, which will eventually reach a critical point. This wobble will cause the top to pivot and re-center its axis so it reorients towards the horizontal belt. In terms of the planet, the greater mass weight of the polar ice will shift towards the equatorial spin.

Does the length of the day change after a polar shift? If there is a change, what is the percent?
If the cataclysm is so intense the planet's orbit is thrown out of kilter, there can be some fluctuation of revolution length until the upheaval settles. Then the day and night hours again become relatively the same unless the planetary orbit has been altered.

But that would involve an interaction with some other body besides the earth.
Very most likely.

Should we consider the effect of the moon and the sun's gravity field in this calculation? In other words, there can be a dipole moment on the earth due to the asymmetrical mass distributions, the earth not being a spherical object.
That is a factor to consider.

An important factor?
The moon has an important aspect in this. We hesitate to give you the details, but your satellite, this Mother's satellite (moon) has not

always been there.

That is interesting. When did it arrive?
Ninety three thousand years previous to this Now.

Right now the Earth's rotation speed is about 1000 miles per hour on the surface, at the equator, relative to its axis of rotation. During a polar shift, you stated, speeds up to 2700 miles per hour were attained. Thus the maximum difference in the kinetic energy before and during a shift is (2.7*2.7 -1.0 = 6.3) about six times the current crust kinetic energy. This energy must be added from some source. Where does this energy come from?
From within the planets reserves, itself. This may be nearly impossible to establish in terms of mathematics.   However, the accumulation of Negative energy contributes to the speed increase also. In the polar shift process, the energy or contaminants intolerable to the Planet's health are neutralized. The negativity is the energy source the Mother uses to increase shis speed and in the process neutralizes those factors which are unbalanced and unhealthy. Therefore, you might be able to say that all nuclear chemical refuse, which is waste and discarded, is fuel which is used by the planet to rebalance. And the waste is used and neutralized in the process.

This is beyond the known laws of dynamics that we understand.
Remember, the weight buildup at the poles, being so uneven, causes the wobble gradually to increase. In terms of mechanics, the inertia wobble force contributes to greater speed during the shift.

Let us ask you another question for clarity. If the inertia force creates a wobble and the build up of the poles increases the frequency and amplitude of the wobble, then there must be a point where this other source of energy kicks in, and with the inertia force causes the crust to break loose and start its slide. Is this correct?
It is not incorrect.

But it would be misleading.
It is not misleading.

How is the stored energy applied to the crust? Is it applied to accelerate a volume of material, like a body force or an external force? A body force is applied throughout the material whereas an

external force is applied on the surface. Is it a body force or a surface force?

It is a combination. This may seem trite, but think of a horse fly on a horse. When the irritation becomes too great, there is a rippling along the horse's musculature which causes the fly to leave. It is a similar combination of forces. The initial trigger is in the whole of the Mothers' body, from within outward. However, the irritant comes from Negative energy on the surface.

Once the crust has accelerated to this velocity, that energy must be dissipated, since the motion eventually stops. The energy is dissipated. Does it go into heat, friction, or in another way?

It is dissipated in many forms.

What is the dominate form? Is it fluid drag?

It is electrical venting. This can alleviate the greatest quantity of negative with least amount of damage.

When you say electrical, do you mean in accordance with our known laws of electromagnetics?

It is Fusion. Lightning. Lightning is fusion, cold fusion.

Yes. We discussed that in the Technology chapter. The next question is more of the social type. From your perspective, is it probable that a substantial portion of our scientific community will accept the idea of polar shifts within the next twenty years or so, or is this very unlikely?

It is quite probable, most probable.

Tao Song.

POLAR SHIFT MANAGEMENT

There is a question regarding the greenhouse effect. There is controversy among scientists regarding the effect of increased carbon dioxide and other pollutants in the atmosphere. Some feel that warming will cause the polar caps to melt.
Which will immediately cool everything off considerably.

And therefore we end up with more ice on the poles? I do not understand that. Can you explain how it works?
It works like a refrigerator.

It works like a refrigerator?
Correct. At this Now, people's consciousness is being focused because of the greenhouse threat. This new awareness is creating very Positive results. It is essential to effect extensive polar ice melt. The increase in carbon dioxide is not a detriment. The increased amounts of carbon dioxide are essential. People will find breathing more difficult. That is what will awaken the people to the need for more atmospheric life preservers: TREES. Because of the global warming, people will attune to the imperative and acute need to increase the tree population. This in itself will rectify the excess of carbon dioxide. This situation has great potential to create a large planetary healing action and afford humans more time to insert themselves once again into the System Balance of the Mother without having to experience a shift. The polar axis wobble will be much less when the ice caps have melted. The melting will in turn introduce more fresh water into the oceans and cause cooling. The cooling will cause more rains. In the end: Better ecological Balance. The greatest potential assistance in coming is the Gahtai, the People in coming. The extraterrestrial triumvirate will instruct Earth humans in polar management. Then the plant, water, and animal Balance can be available to Earth human technology, in terms of how these factors correlate to ice cap build up and control. These events have great potential for occurring within thirty to fifty linear years.

This is interesting. It is wonderful to think that we will develop an active technology to assist in polar cap management with the assistance of ET's.
We wish to offer this, once again. The intent for this Mother

Planet's function is that Spiritual advancement and Technological advancement be reflective of each other. Therefore, the more advanced the spirituality, the more advanced the technology. If either one becomes out of "sync" problems arise. So, it is important to state in this book that technology and spirituality must walk hand in hand as friends.

Many people who are wholistic in their approach to science and technology have an aversion to the assumptions and methods of traditional scientists. Science has offended them to some extent. Perhaps traditional scientists feel the same way about people who subscribe to metaphysics and wholistics.
It is important for all who have this suspicious attitude to rethink themselves. Remember that those actions, thoughts, or beliefs which are divisive are detrimental. Those actions which include or embrace are Positive. For instance, if there is a willingness to make the best product, considering all materials available, using all knowledge and methods available, then it is most likely that the product will be excellent and Balanced. It is the same with information and knowledge. The intent behind the thought and action influences the outcome of any action.

Edgar Cayce, in 1934, predicted changes you are talking about. It sounds very much like a polar shift. Cayce projected these occurrences in the period from 1958 and 1998. Obviously things have changed. At the time Cayce read the projections from the Akashic records, the probabilities projected a polar shift in the middle of the second half of this century. It has moved out in time. Something has changed the date. What changed the date?
The projection has changed because a number of the Followers of the Law of One chose to reincarnate at a time which would have them function as adults in this Now. A very great number of the Followers of the Law of One were born during the years 1935 to 1955. Their choice was to reenter the Physical Plane in order to avert the catastrophe of a polar shift and assist in another attempt at The Jump. Followers of the Law of One have been working together to achieve Balance and the Rate or Dimension increase in all similar situations, in all other circles of civilizations.

How many Followers of the Law of One reincarnated in the period between 1935 and 1955?
Nearly two hundred fifty thousand. This does not seem to be

many. However, when you think that each Follower of the Law of One, working with Positive intent, can carry seven other people towards Positive, this multiplies the potential for Balance immensely. Thought energy when applied in a Positive group and with a specific intent carries seven to the seventh power force for Balance. This occurrence caused the change, the reprieve you might say.

Seven to seventh power is a large number (823,543). That is wonderful. Not only do the polar shifts depend on how we harmonize with the planet, but to a great extent it depends on how we harmonize with each other. Correct?

Exactly. It is the intent. It is purposefully using Beneficial Wholism Assessment for the Mother. Positive intent influences the extension of the linear time interval between shifts, even the probabilities of a shift. Polar shifts are a combination of mechanics and Metaphysics. This may cause the scientific community considerable difficulty.

Is the intent of the humans today in "Consideration" with the planets intended functions?

When there is conflicting intent between the humans and the Mother then imbalance ensues. When the intent is to use the Planet simply for the resources shis can offer, as opposed to accepting and caring for the Mother as you care for yourselves, then the accumulated Negative energy produced by this conflict of intent leads to a polar shift if it is not rectified.

As we have stated previously, the plan for humans on this Mother is two fold. It is to achieve a highly advanced global technology, and to have that technology be in Balance with the Mother and shis living systems. As long as these two factors remain, Balanced polar shifts can be avoided. You see, humans are not only learning inter-system harmony, they are also learning that as Creators of their own reality and environment, they are required to become Planet Managers in order to prevent further polar shifts. You will learn to manage the poles, monitor the weight of the masses of ice, and develop the technology to resolve polar cap buildup without damaging any of the Mother systems. When all human intent is toward Positive, planet management of all life, including the Mother shiself, as a single organism, will prevent further polar shifts.

Tao Song.

HELP FROM E.T.'s

Many people believe in the existence of extraterrestrials. Are there E.T.s here today.?

There is an ensouled species resident on this Mother which is not indigenous. They are Travitors[56] who have taken up residency by choice. They are called Freshono.

Where do they live?

In the ocean. The Freshono maintain the inter-galactic transfer station located on this Mother. The Freshono chose to stay on this Mother and ensure that this branch transfer station remains operational. In the beginning, these Travitors were a gas breathing species like yourselves, air breathing. The original Travitors interbred with a liquid breathing species resident in the Mother's oceans. The new generation of the hybrid species are completely adapted to deep ocean conditions and need no alternate residence or environment. The Freshono, being a combination species, can breathe both air and water. The legends of Mer people, mermaids, are based on young Freshono pranksters. Many of the adolescent Freshono thought it was quite a joke to station themselves upon rocks or shoals and then drop their shields for sailors, thus giving the impression of appearing out of nowhere and then disappearing. Aquatic "flashers," so to speak. This game was completely discouraged by the adult Freshono long ago, in terms of linear time. However, since many Terrans saw the Freshono youths, the accounts still exist in the Mythology of Terrans. The smile[57] is that, in actuality, it is not myth but reality. The Freshono have a highly advanced water technology. They can control water. They can manipulate water at a molecular level. They can create buildings from water. They have the ability to stabilize water, use water for many different things - for tools, buildings, light sources. It is complex.

It is quite a bit beyond our technical understanding to do those things.

---

[56]Travitor - This is a composite term for traveler-visitor.

[57]Joke or humor.

Freshono technology was developed with the assistance of certain mechanicals which were brought when the first Travitors decided to remain.

When was that?
The Travitors first agreed to this assignment some 650,000 years ago. The last of the original Extraterrestrial species passed[58] five hundred years after the first group established residency. By that time, there were two hundred successful hybrid pairs in existence to continue the colony. There are only two hundred thousand individuals present on this Mother at this Now.

It sounds like they are not interested in letting us know where they are located.
The Freshono are not anxious that their locations be discovered. The population of the Freshono is quite small and entirely peaceful. They have the ability to observe the behavior of Terrans and are not inclined to trust that human character and motives are benign because the Freshono are so vulnerable. Because of this, they guard their existence and their city with diligence. They do this with their water technology. The Freshono can manipulate water in order to disguise their location.

If we make The Jump to Mind Mechanics, we will be an expanded society and they will no longer need to have such concerns.
Correct.

Is there anything else?
We can give this as a small uplift. There is much concern over ocean canisters of wastes which we discussed previously. There are some developments the Freshono are working on to seal off some of the more dangerously deteriorating canisters.

That is great. Are they working with the whales on this?
The whales report to the Freshono the location and quantity of waste canisters and their condition of stability, Yes.

Once they are located the Freshono can do something about it.

---

[58]passed- passed on, died

Correct.

That is great. We had not thought of that. If it was dependant upon us, it would be a while. It is difficult for the people who live on land to get going on a project of that magnitude in the ocean.
 Take heart. There is, even as we speak, a large project in the planning regarding just these factors.

What is an inter-galactic transfer station?
 It is a switching station for commerce, for Rate or Dimension adjustments for travelers. But mostly it is for tourists.

You mentioned that we will be receiving help from "others" that are greatly concerned with our Mother's environmental situation.
 Correct.

What is the form of this assistance?
 It is bio-resolution, eco-resolution on a planetary scale. There will be ocean purifying processes introduced. The "People" incoming can offer efficient and non-degenerative air purifying processes including the resolve of the Planet's atmospheric envelope. They can offer instruction regarding weather management. Also, the clarification of human's function and their importance not only to this Mother but to other functioning planetary Systems which have sapient life. There are many other areas of assistance. These are but a few. The "People" need only be assured of your trust and your effort to try to accomplish these things for yourselves. The "People" incoming can not give you assistance if there is a desire or an attempt to obliterate them. Therefore, at this Now, only circumspect assistance is occurring. Much assistance and information is being given on an individual level. These assisted persons can then encourage others to trust and not fear assistance from E.T.s.

You mentioned that the Earth is part of a triad of planets, one of three. What is that connection all about?
 Functioning units are in threes. There are three systems which Balance each other. The triad of planets is from one system. The Gahtai is a consortium of "People" from three planets of another system which are coming to assist this Mother. This Mother Planet is a single System Unit shiself. All three Systems must be Balanced. We will not discuss the third system, however. A System can be one planet or

many.

Discussion regarding the "People" incoming can become somewhat confusing when trying to establish place, number and time.

Are there many technical civilizations in the galaxy at this Now? Are there hundreds, thousands, or millions of such planets?

Were you speaking of this specific galaxy you call Milky Way?

Yes.

Do you mean separate planets on which there is sapient life and technological development?

Yes.

There are thousands of inhabited systems. The Balanced Triad in this quadrant contains one hundred three inhabited planets with a developed technology.

You might say what defines the boundaries of the quadrant.

This "quadrant" is defined in more complex terms than mathematical or spacial. The area is designated, space wise, upon available raw material. That is why this Mother is so essential to all other Systems within the quadrant. When one element within a System is out of Balance, the entire System becomes out of Balance. This in turn puts the quadrant out of Balance and affects the sector in which the quadrant resides, etc. This extends to the sector and this Galaxy as a whole.

Is that why there is a great "off-planet" interest in our situation? Because all are tied to each other?

Correct.   And one Law of the Physical Plane Universe is: **Balance will not occur if any sapient beings desert their neighbors in time of need.**

Are the E.T.s that visit us from our own galaxy or from other galaxies?

In previous times, there have been some visitors from other galaxies, even from other Universes. However, most of the physical activities and assistance at this Now come from beings within your own system. Not your solar system, but the System Triad of which you are one part. They are from your Quadrant.

When you say beings from other Universes, our known concept of the Universe is it is 15 billion light years across and there is only one.   Where are these other Universes located, in another dimension?

This concept of "Universe" which you describe comes from an incomplete understanding of the geometrical structure. This leads to confusion. There are three Universes within the Physical Plane. The way to comprehend this is to say they are different in dimension or Rate.

Will the greater majority of the world's population be informed that beings from other planets will come to assist us to clean up the pollution which exists on our Mother?

Eventually, when the "People" know that their lives and help will not be responded to with fear and violence, Yes. The necessity of having the majority informed is essential. That is what you are all working towards.

Tao Song.

ENERGIZING POSITIVE ACTION

Can you give a hypothetical description of a Balanced technological society and how the basic systems work - energy, water, sewage, transportation, and agriculture?
You are asking for the "whole ball of wax", so speak. We would wish to offer you this. The key factor to be aware of is that in a Balanced society each individual is aware, from moment to moment, of exactly that which Balance **IS**. In other words, each individual is aware of what to do and what not to do in order to augment their interaction with the planetary processes which are existent. Therefore, that of which you have spoken, meaning the condition of water, of technology, of air, of human interaction, of energy systems would be those which with the use of Beneficial Wholism Assessment would be the most Positive. Now, to give a more specific outline, the natural non-polluting Positive augmenting energy system within this solar system and of course this Mother is solar energy. The development and perfection of efficient solar energy is the first major technological advancement to be aware of. It is not possible to continue to use non-renewable fossil fuels and remain in Balance with this Mother and shis operating systems. The subsequential technology, in terms of technology which requires energy to operate, would be based upon solar energy. The most effectively Balanced soil-water-air functioning would be the normalizing of the "in process" system; the natural process and system of the Mother shiself. In many instances the acceleration of technology to insure that the return to as Natural a functioning as possible within the system of functioning systems is and would be required. Balance within human interaction would be the inherent intent. That all humans augment the potentials of thought, action, and accomplishment of each other. Taking into consideration that there is always the potential for the chaos factor, for the aberrant, but considering that aspect with the intent to deal with the chaos factor in the most Balanced Wholisticaly Assessed means possible. In a Balanced society there will occur more intimate interaction between humans and themselves, and the Mother's material self and humans. In a Balanced society there is also the potential for accelerated inter-species communication - communication between Enedswr species and also hive species. The Balanced society will "Consider" each aspect and action taken. The singular decision of any individual and the majority decision of the masses will be in accord.

The technicalities which so weigh this Now society down will seem as feathers to brush away. That which makes work in a Balanced society will be that which augments the Whole. You will find that there is no longer any value placed in money, what we have called "metal". Those things of value and honor will be the **ideal** followed by those who can put the **ideal** into function and make the **ideal** a material reality. The individual worth will not be a question. Each human, each Enedswr will have shis place, not place meaning cast, but place meaning contribution and all others will have honor and admiration of those persons' contributions, and function, and place. We are speaking in large generalities. Do you wish to ask for specifics?

Yesterday we were walking in a stream in the state forest and I realized that drinking the water would be a health risk. In the future Balanced world, that same stream will be almost undisturbed by man so that scooping up a glass of water to drink will be no problem.

Dear one, the important factor to understand is that the stream will most likely be greatly disturbed by man. However, in their great honor, their disturbing of that stream will not be offensive, but recreational. Yes, many glasses can be scooped and drunk. Many immersings, many swimmings, many splashings and pleasures may occur because the same honor will be given to the stream as there is honor given to the human being. The Oneness will be recognized.

What about the population density and the total number of people. You have already touched upon the relationship between people and Nature and each other. What about the shear magnitude of the numbers of people in a Balanced society?

In a Balanced society the remembering of Balanced control of conception will occur. Therefore the possibility of population pressure through numbers will be neutralized. When there is the remembering of perpetuation instead of procreation from fear, the conception and population accordingly will be in Balance with all other species on this Mother. In other words, if there is "numbers pressure" humans will simply not conceive. This is a quite a stretchy concept and risky to speak of in this Now. It is the Souls power to regulate Hive-House procreation. When it is in **Balance** for the Mother and the species to multiply, that function will function.

What can an individual do to create Positive action?

One of the most crucial and Beneficial actions any individual can take is to note shis thought process. Not only what shis thinks, but how the thinking process functions and the thoughts that are conceived. It is a great Positive action to observe how thought processes mold decisions which subsequently determine choices for action.

This may seem abstract, but the foundation of Positive energy production is Positive Consideration. To think and learn Consideration, a person must analyze and understand what the word "consider" really means. It is a process - assessing and observing all that occurs within a "System" and what can potentially occur within a "System." If you have a Balanced, Considerate thought process, the decisions at which you arrive, and the actions you choose, will automatically be Positive ones producing Positive outcomes.

The process of generating energy is Thought=Decision=Action. When the individual recognizes the process itself and truly "Considers" that process, then the greatest move towards Positive energy production occurs. Now, Positive Consideration of the thought process leads to what we call "Beneficial Wholism Assessment." This is the "action" aspect of any process. People who use Beneficial Wholism Assessment train their thought processes first. **Beneficial Wholism Assessment energizes a person's desire to ensure shis decisions and actions create the most harmonic environment possible for the Mother planet and shis living systems.**

Your thoughts and self assessments are included in the function of the Planetary System. Consider this. Is your thinking respectful to the part you are within the system? Remember, all systems and beings are linked together. If you think "Considerately" about yourselves, you are applying Beneficial Wholism Assessment with regard to your part of the whole system. Self Consideration is the first action. This is the stone thrown into the pool of water creating ever-expanding ripples. Each subsequent reassessment, reexamination, reconsideration of a Thought=Decision=Action continues a process which assures that no discord or imbalance occurs for all interrelated links within your system. The choice of each individual to employ Beneficial Wholism Assessment is the embodiment of "Consideration."

When you decide to do a thing based upon Consideration, examining all potential factors that your action may have upon all parts of the system within which you function, you can say, "I am practicing Beneficial Wholism Assessment. I am observing my thoughts and attempting to assure that my actions will be only those which create a continuous Positive ripple." Then you will have achieved the most

Positively energized action possible.

Many may think this seems too esoteric, not very pragmatic; but those who initiate Beneficial Wholism Assessment in their thoughts first, next in their decisions, and finally in their actions, will never be faced with questions of morality such as, "Is it right to kill this whale or cut this tree?" Their action will never be in conflict with System Consideration. It would be impossible to act in any other manner than one which is Harmonic and Balanced. There would be no question as to whether or not a polluting technology was valid. Eventually there would be no difference between Balanced thought, System Consideration, and Balanced action. It would be impossible to think a thought which was out of Balance or detrimental to any other part of the living system.

It is important to become comfortable with never being quite sure, become comfortable with reassessing from moment to moment the possibilities and potentials of ones thoughts, decisions, or actions. In other words, learn immediate and incredible flexibility. Ask yourselves, Dear Ones, constantly, "Will this be Beneficial and contribute to myself, to those I love, to my trees, my oceans? Will this thought and action be good for the air I breathe, for the other living beings that share my Home, this Planet? Will my action be good in this moment? Will it be Beneficial tomorrow and next month and a year from now?" If every person assesses with Consideration their thought, decisions, and then their actions, moment to moment, and receives from within feelings of **Rightness** and **Yes** answers to those questions, then they will be practicing Beneficial Wholism Assessment. Of course Consideration can be applied to many small tasks, single practical actions, also. You can ask, "How will I feel if I plant this tree? Is it good for the earth? Is it good for the air? Is it smiley for all the other living creatures?" You will have a Yes answer. That is a Positive contribution. If you throw some wild flower seeds from the car window as you go for a drive, is that a Beneficially Assessed action? Of course. If you are sure that your automobiles are running at peak efficiency and are serviced and are as non-polluting as possible at this Now, then is that a Beneficially Wholistic action. Yes. There are many actions which may seem small and unimportant but can create great Positive collectively. It is the intent, based in Consideration, behind the action which creates the Positive healing of this Mother. It is the choice to practice coordination - Considered thoughts and Considered actions - until it becomes natural and spontaneous. These practices will accomplish Balance for all Systems of this Mother.

You say that intention has much to do with the outcome of any considered decision. For example, suppose a person was planning on building a deck, which I did. In the process of doing that I said to myself, "I think that using Redwood will be attractive and also cost effective." I then built a Redwood deck. That was the process that occurred at the time. At this point, I might re-think the situation using Beneficial Wholism Assessment and I would say, "I would like a deck, and I would like a Redwood deck, but a Redwood deck might not be so beneficial because a wood deck means buying Redwood lumber, and that means cutting trees. So perhaps an alternate material could be considered, a brick or a stone patio" - something along those lines.

Correct. This method of thought amalgamation is the start of Beneficial Wholism Assessment. The application of the Considerate thought process is the practice of Beneficial Wholism Assessment. Using this process prior to decision and prior to action - that is the key. Then you are wanting to choose, intending to choose, and enacting only those actions which meet the requirements for creative Positive and Balance for all things within your system. You can give yourself the joy of a patio without having to cause imbalance in any of the Mother's living Systems. That is what epitomizes the process of Beneficial Wholism Assessment. Performing only those actions backed by Positive Intent.

Suppose in the previous example, that after assessing the situation and considering all the factors, for various reasons, the decision was to build the Redwood deck - the same decision which was previously arrived at without Beneficial Wholism Assessment. Is there a significant difference between those two approaches which result in the same action? Intuition suggests there is.

That is correct. There is a definite difference. How could you, however, with the use of Beneficial Wholism Assessment, arrive at that choice?

Based on that premise, it would not be possible.

Exactly.

There are those who could arrive at that choice. How can we say full Consideration was not given?

We wish to offer you this. The very example you have given is why we stated that the most significant action to take in this Now, the key to all other actions, is to think about how you think. Retrain the thought processes so that there is no other alternative than that of using Beneficial Wholism Assessment. It is the thought retraining which is the primary action, the essential action to take in this Now.

How does an individual facilitate that within shiself?

Practice speaking out loud. Play a game with yourself. Say that today you are going to count how many "always" that you say or "can'ts" or "shoulds" or other confining and divisive words or concepts of thought. Count how many of these you use and how often you use them. How many Negative thoughts? How many self-undermining statements or thoughts have you made? By observing what you think about yourself and how often it is thought you can learn "attention." Paying acute attention then affords the individual the opportunity to make a conscious choice - to choose what kind of thoughts are wanted. Of course the retraining cannot be done in one day, but the practice is an action which points out, "There. You thought it again. You said it again. We are not thinking in this manner anymore." Then the individual begins to replace constricted and divisive words and thoughts with Positive Considered thoughts. And speaking aloud greatly assists in thought retraining.

That gets back to personal growth.

Exactly. But paying attention and speaking aloud is Positive action. It is the first step which will energize the healing of the Mother because that action can unify the intent of human beings as a Whole.

So then, the process of each individual rethinking how he or she thinks, assists the larger Whole to accelerate at an even greater pace than that of a single individual. When a group of people thinks along the same lines, the thought energy is much stronger.

We send you applause.

The line of thinking that we want to initiate is: In order to achieve Planetary Balance we first achieve personal Balance. Anything that achieves personal Balance is a beneficial contribution to the Balance of the Whole.

However, there must be the choice, the decision to put what is learned from within into practical outside application. Thinking can not be active spiritual growth if it is only intellectual, only mental recognition of where growth is needed. **True personal growth is:**

Application of what is learned. Therefore, the choice to assist yourself to grow must be the initial step. Followed by action, it allows all others to grow also. If you decide that you do not like to see trees cut, take no action which will require the cutting of trees. It is the outside application of inner thought which constitutes growth. That is true knowledge. That is action. That is creative contribution.

Doesn't each Soul inherently have knowledge of Balance?
The Soul not only knows Balance, but is Balance. But, as you all have experienced at times, it is very dificult to see and be Balance when contending with existence in a Physical body and a Physical Universe. For some, Balance is clear. There is harmony with the Soul-Self more often than not. However, at times, many need to perceive Balance in the Physical Plane with their Physical bodies in order to remember that that potential IS, and is within All.

Energizing thoughts into action.
Correct.

Energizing Positive action.
Exactly. Start allowing yourselves to relearn yourselves and your thinking. Then initiate pragmatic action based upon what has been learned. The Positive Intent is important, but if the intent is only supported with lip service, it is not as powerful. Intent becomes Energized Positive when put into **action**.

Can you give us an example, a somewhat elaborate example, a somewhat complicated scenario involving Beneficial Wholism Assessment? You previously mentioned decisions on cutting a tree. How about something tricky like whether or not to build a freeway bypass around a town, about the associated routes, alternatives and so on to be assessed in that process. Within the process people have opportunities to attend meetings, express opinions, become involved, and become educated.
Correct.

This would be a realistic and complex example. It would be a tangible example since there are many communities facing this issue.
Many complex issues can become less complicated if the Primary Priority is kept clearly in the foreground. First: Determine the

objective to be accomplished.   In terms of Beneficial Wholism Assessment, does it accomplish the objective, without sacrificing or putting in jeopardy the integrity of the living systems.   Therefore, although technically and financially challenging, the Primary Priority is to accomplish the objective without environmental interference. Often people allow technicalities to interfere with the Primary Priority.

What does the majority want? Understand, though we speak in general terms in this instance, it is possible to "have your cake and eat it too." It is possible to plan and build a bypass without interfering or contributing to the degeneration of the surrounding environment. It is not a matter of whether or not it is feasible. It is a question of whether there is a willingness not to allow technicalities to side track the Primary objective. Are the people willing to sacrifice Consideration and simply do what is quickest, least costly, and easy, or are the people willing to use Beneficial Wholism Assessment? There are definitely pressures and financial Considerations, especially for those who have financial interests foremost in their desires. Many communities as a group have managed to thwart the radical and inconsiderate bypass designs.   Remember, there is a way to accomplish the objective without sacrificing the Primary Priority - Balance.   The essential factor in this instance is discerning what is the most Considerate action to take, and deciding as a group that whatever is required to accomplish the objective in Balance will be done, regardless of the cost pressure or advantage.

All an individual can do is stand by shis own Positive Considerations, seek out those who have the same, who will seek out more who have the same. Refuse to be compromised or compromise. Work to find individuals who either have methods or information to help deal with the technicalities and still adhere to the Primary Priority. Seek out those who will use Beneficial Wholism Assessment; those who will carefully assess each new issue or factor involved in the project and yet not lose site of the Primary objective which in this case is: Providing a freeway bypass without endangering the living systems of the area.

In this case, what are some of those Considerations to be included?
Many similar situations require making sure that precise and extensive factual information regarding intent and purpose are always up to date and available so that there are no ways to hide ulterior motives.

These are important. I was hoping for something a little more tangible in this case.
At times becoming overly specific could cause influence and

also invite aggressive attention to the questioner. Therefore we, with respect, are not allowed to continue with this example. You may proceed with your train of thought, however.

There are many factors to be considered and it is quite complicated. There are the environmental considerations of the various alternatives for the ecology of the area. There are economic impacts, the "quality of life" impacts on the people adjacent to prospective routes. There is the impact of the no bypass option; there are also alternatives to freeways such as two lane roads and boulevards. These are the type of factors that people are talking about. There are also the quality of the studies which support the assessment of these impacts. And, of course, in addition to this there are all the different personal preferences and what we call the "not in my back yard" syndrome.
> Correct. Please continue.

There are people saying that there is a need to look at the impact on local traffic problems. There are people saying that there is a responsibility to the state-wide transportation system and its problems in facilitating inter-regional transportation. This goes on and on.
> You have discovered the heart of the issue, so to speak. In a "backyard" kind of community no matter where this bypass goes it is going to be "in the back yard." Therefore, the issue must be discussed as a community and decided as a community. The question to be asked as a community is, "Do we want this in our back yard?"

Right.
> What is your responsibility to the state transportation system? It is your "back yard." These are the Considerations. It is difficult to use specific "what to do's" because each individual has individual interest. But, priorities are essential when employing the process of Beneficial Wholism Assessment in order to insure that your part of the Whole's "back yard" is not put into a condition of imbalance.

Yes instead of thinking I live on the west side or the east side, I could think of the area as a whole.
> Yes. Thinking: "This valley is my back yard."

Thinking, "I live in this valley, which is my back yard. What is

going to happen to this valley?"
Exactly.

I can definitely see the benefit of making that one unifying leap.
Correct. It is prioritizing the goal. Focused, clear, thought to the priority will make the process of Beneficial Wholism Assessment much simpler. Ask yourself, "Is it good for me, is it good for my neighbor? Is it good for our valley? Is it good for the trees and the living systems of this area?" What about this area's impact on the Planet if this is in "my back yard"? Do you see?

Yes.
And then decide whether construction can be accomplished without negative occurring within the system. If a choice is made to keep the priorities in Balance then a way will be found. It is always possible to resolve any issue; accomplish any idea Beneficially for all. If a Balanced resolve is not possible, the issue is even more simple. Do not undertake the project.

In fifty words or less what can you say to those who want to energize Positive action.
First: Clarify the Priority. Ask yourselves, "What do I want to do?" Then do what brings Joy and Balance, and contributes to All you encounter. Even the smallest action, a greeting, a smile, reaching out to pat a tree, admire a flower, or care for a small hive animal is Positive Action. Start by encouraging the Positive within yourselves and believing in the power you have as an individual.

Tao Song.

WHICH WAY THE WIND BLOWS

We have discussed many topics together. We have spoken of your hopes, ideals and potentials for this Mother. We have given many pieces of factual information that some will deem conjecture or guess work. As to these facts, some are substantiable, others will become so in time. Many will possibly remain un-substantiated for a long period of linear time. Each individual must reach within shiself and trust what is felt rightly in regards to the stretchy factual material. The individual, after all, is the Creator within whose hand the outcome, well being, and Positive enlivening of this Mother is held.

We wish to assure you that at this Now the Mother is not past the "point of no return." Balance is possible. Humans can unify and heal the injuries that you have inflicted on yourselves and your Mother Planet. Many may become bowed under stones of discouragement, thinking, that as individuals it is not possible to do enough soon enough to salvage the Mother let alone turn the environmental condition around. We wish to assure you that this is not the case. It is important for you to believe in yourselves and in your power. All actions start with the individual. And it is the decision of one individual to act that influences another, that influences two, who influence four and so on. The combined action magnifies and intensifies the original individual's power in degrees that you can not possibly imagine. It is first: Belief in yourselves which makes a Balanced Environment a Reality. In the Physical Plane, avenues of possibility are never closed. There is always a solution to resolve error and create Positive for Balance. There is never any error too great, short of planetary disintegration of course, that cannot be resolved.

We wish to again remind you of the power of your individual thought energy. **You create what you think.** Think about the content of your thoughts. Question what you believe and why you hold those beliefs. Belief systems are tools to assist you in your creative process. You cannot create your ideal using broken or worn tools. If the tools you are using are creating discord and imbalance, make new tools. Think about what you want. Energize the Balanced outcome. Fill your thoughts, your mind, and spirit with visions of a healed planet. See the environment in your thoughts as a crisis resolved; one which you have already healed. We do not, of course, mean to sit on your Laurels in inaction, but see every action you do take to heal the Mother as the ultimate healing action. We do not say these things as criticism. We are speaking of this to empower you as individuals - to assist you to remember what you already know. **ALL IS ONE.** You have heard this many times before. Believe that you are connected and that your life, your Environment, your Planet, and your Universe are inseparable, for it is true. This is the key. Realize that the individual and shis action has the power to affect The Whole. So give yourself health, nurturing, patience, and understanding, knowing as you do so that these are things that then automatically flow from you to the Whole itself. Take actions which "Honor Life," for yourself, for your area, and for your world. Believe that when you ask for clarity, you will receive clarity. Know that Right Action is: **That which Augments All Living Beings.**

We have confidence in your potential and your power. So think of what you want and leave what you do not want out of your thinking. Practice Consideration through the use of Beneficial Wholism Assessment. When you begin to recreate your thoughts in Balance you will be well on the road to Harmony with the Mother.

Avoid triggering the Law of Resistance.[59] If you initiate protest and prevention - setting yourself against a thing which is already done - your energy investment only empowers what you are struggling to prevent. Therefore do not waste your creative energy railing. Go and take action which moves the Mother towards Balance.

You are all Creators for The Tao. You create well.
Create Life and all will be Life. You cannot be defeated.

Tao Song.

---

[59]The Law of Resistance - That which you resist you draw to yourself and make your reality. That which you pursue in anguish or anxiety will elude you.

Dedication

This project is dedicated to the Mother Planet
and to all the Followers of the Law of One
working to insure Balance.

About the cover

The symbol on the front cover was used by the Followers of the Law of
One to repesent Balance with Nature during the Golden Age of the
previous advanced civilization - the Athlenta civilization. The blue,
white, and green energy bands in front of the Mother planet represent
Balance for the ocean, the atmosphere, and the land respectively. The
wave symbolizes attunement. The slightly different symbol on the back
of the book represents prospective Balance for the current civilzation -
the Kham civilization.

TAO SONG

ORDERS

Conversations With Tomorrow - Achieving Environmental Balance can be ordered from:

> CDC Publishing
> 216 Redwood Avenue
> Willits, California 95490
>
> Fax 707-459-0241
>
> Phone 707-459-0245

Please include a check with your order. Books can be returned for a full refund - for any reason, no questions asked.

Shipping:
Book rate: Shipping within the continetal United States is $1.50.

Sales tax:
Please include sales tax for books shipped to a California address.

Price:
The book price is $14.95 per copy. The price with $1.50 for shipping is $16.45. The price with both shipping and $1.05 California sales tax is $17.50.